1000 Answers: What Everyone Should Know About Stuttering

David Alpuche

Praise for 1000 Answers

"David has written an inspiring chronicle of his lifelong journey as a person who stutters. His entertaining account of his experiences intertwined with the scientific knowledge he has gained about stuttering will educate, inform, and engage the reader. This is a 'must read' for everyone interested in stuttering and those who enjoy personal stories about how individuals deal with challenges." – **Janice Lougeay**, Professor of Practice, University of Texas at Dallas.

"As a longtime professor and researcher of stuttering, I can say this book provides incredible insight into the human experience of stuttering. Not only are the perspectives of many experts (people who stutter) shared, but much of the commentary is synthesized with high-quality, educational information. This book is an engaging, informative resource that could supplement clinical and academic activities." – **Angela M. Medina**, PhD, CCC-SLP.

"David communicates his experience and knowledge about stuttering in a way that is candid, accessible, vulnerable, and even humorous. This book should be required reading for speech pathologists." – **Toya Harris**, Director of Education at To Be Like Me.

"David Alpuche has accomplished the herculean task of creating an informational and emotional road map about stuttering. He relates his experiences with stuttering with incisiveness, humor, emotion, objectivity, and artfulness. The inclusion of many perspectives lends the book an unbiased window into the many that stuttering can impact one's life." – **John Gomez**, Speech-Language Pathologist and Filmmaker.

"By sharing some of his personal journey and experiential knowledge, along with others affected by stuttering, David answers some of the many questions we are routinely asked by parents, students, and speech-language pathologists about the communication difference we contend with daily. I highly recommend this book to anyone interested in adding to their knowledge about stuttering." - **Lee Reeves**, Former Chairman of the Board of the NSA and person who stutters.

Copyright © 2024 by David Alpuche
All rights reserved.
No part of this publication may be reproduced, distributed, or transmitted in any form, by any means, or stored in a database or retrieval system, without the publisher's prior written permission.

Photographs by David Alpuche
Cover designed by Estefan Cuanalo

ISBN 979-8-9918357-0-1

DDDDDAVID LLC

Russ Hicks and Lee Reeves, 2024

"If I have seen further, it is by standing on the shoulders of giants" — **Sir Isaac Newton.**

**ANYBODY
FROM ANYWHERE
CAN DO ANYTHING**
- TWENTY ONE PILOTS

Table of Contents

Table of Contents	7
Introduction	1
What is stuttering?	7
What causes stuttering?	12
How is stuttering diagnosed?	14
How do you measure "severity"?	16
Does everyone stutter the same?	19
When and how did you first realize that you stutter?	20
How would you explain stuttering to others based on your personal experience?	22
What is the most common feeling you associate with stuttering?	24
What would you want other people to understand about stuttering?	26
What are common misconceptions about stuttering?	28
What was it like in school?	30
How do you handle your stuttering when meeting people for the first time?	35
Did you ever believe that "it would just go away," and when it didn't, how did you cope?	39
Was there a pivotal moment that changed how you viewed stuttering?	41
What advice would you give to individuals who struggle to accept themselves?	46
What advice would you give to a parent of a child who stutters?	50
Do you ever get used to having a stutter?	53
Does stuttering run in your family?	55
Are you aware that you are stuttering when you stutter?	56
Do you frequently get unsolicited "advice" from people who don't stutter? Do you find it condescending or patronizing?	59
Is there something that a communication partner can do to make conversations easier for you?	61
What are some of the techniques you've learned that have helped you the most?	62
How does stuttering affect your social life?	65

How has stuttering affected your intimate relationships? _____ 66

Has stuttering affected your professional life? _____ 70

How has having a stutter affected getting hired for a job? _____ 72

When you talk with others who stutter, does their stuttering influence yours? _ 76

Do you think your life would be drastically different if you didn't stutter? _____ 78

Did stuttering affect your temperament growing up? _____ 81

If you could give your past self advice about stuttering, what would you say? __ 83

Has your view on stuttering and you as a person who stutters changed over the years? If so, how? _____ 86

Have you used the Speech Easy or other devices that "stop" stuttering? _____ 88

Are there medications that help with stuttering? _____ 92

If you could take a magic pill and make your stuttering go away immediately, would you? Why or why not? _____ 94

What's the craziest thing you have tried to eliminate your stutter? _____ 96

Do you stutter in the other languages you speak? _____ 106

What have been the biggest obstacles to overcome regarding stuttering? ____ 108

What are some things you have accomplished despite your stuttering? _____ 111

Do you stutter in your dreams? _____ 117

If you worked with a speech therapist, what did they do well? What do you wish they had done better? _____ 118

Did you ever have a "breakthrough" moment in therapy? _____ 121

What advice would you give future speech pathologists? _____ 125

What support does the National Stuttering Association provide to individuals who stutter? _____ 128

What continuing education opportunities exist for professionals working with individuals who stutter? _____ 131

What resources (books, blogs, websites, etc) have you found helpful? _____ 132

Final thoughts _____ 136

Acknowledgments _____ 138

About the Author _____ 140

Extras _____ 141

Introduction

I hate introductions.

My name is David. I know how to say David. Except every time I try to say my name, it comes out more like D-d-d-d-davvv-v-v-v-v-v-viiid. I am a person who stutters.

You probably have an idea of what stuttering is: Repeating sounds at the beginning of words, hesitations while speaking, trouble making sounds, that sort of thing. You are correct; those are SOME of the characteristics of stuttering, but do you know what goes through the mind of somebody who stutters while they stutter? Do they forget their words? Is it caused by nervousness? Are you born a person who stutters, or can you develop it as an adult? Can you pass it on to your kids? Do you stutter when you sing?

I am a person who stutters, and for most of my life, I didn't have answers to these or many other questions. I didn't even have a clear name for what I had. From the time I started stuttering at two years old until my late 20s, I visited a few psychologists, a psychiatrist, a hypnotist, a neurologist, and even a "witch" that someone recommended. Some people called it stuttering ("tartamudeo" in Spanish, my native tongue), but others said it was *dyskinesia*[1], that I was "just nervous," or that my speech was just a side effect of trauma. This left me feeling hopeless and perplexed by my inability to speak "normally." As I grew up, the questions piled up, but a

---

[1] "Dyskinesia" is a general term to describe uncontrollable and involuntary movements. It's when your body moves in ways you cannot control. It can affect just one body part, like the head or an arm, or your entire body.

shrug was my best answer when somebody asked me why I talked this way. Stuttering is so complex that even people who stutter are confused by it.

This started to change one day in 2011. I'm 29 years old. I work cleaning tables at a restaurant. This is far from my dream job. It's the kind of job you have when you don't want to talk to anybody, the kind of job you take because you are scared to do anything else.

I was walking around the restaurant when Linda, one of our regulars, asked me to come to her table. I walked there, and she asked me if it would be okay if she looked for somebody to help me with my speech. It wasn't the first time we talked about my stutter, but it caught me off guard. I didn't have time to think about it, so I said yes, after which she asked me to write my name and email on a piece of paper. I would've never guessed it, but that moment would change my life forever.

A few days later, I received an email from her telling me that she found Dr. Frances Freeman at the University of Texas at Dallas (UTD) and that she had agreed to meet me. "This is her number; call *her*," read the email.

Oh yeah, I will pick up the phone and call a stranger. If I were on Family Feud and the question was "Things People Who Stutter Are Terrified Of," I would bet the house and everything I own on "phone calls" would be in the top 3. It took me weeks to convince myself to call that number. When I finally gathered the courage to make the call, the voice on the other side was sweet and patient. She asked me questions I struggled to answer, but we had an appointment by the end of the call.

Dr. Freeman turned out to be a godsend. Over the next few months, she helped demystify stuttering for me. She taught me that stuttering was even more complicated than

I thought but also not that big of a deal. It was unfortunate, but it was just a tiny part of me, and it didn't have to control my life. It wasn't my fault.

Dr. Freeman helped me enormously, but her most significant contribution to my life might have been introducing me to the National Stuttering Association (NSA). It's hard to understand why, but I had never met another person who stuttered before attending their meetings. At first, I did not like talking to other people who stuttered. I realized that if I didn't stutter myself, I would probably freak out and wouldn't know how to react if some stranger started stuttering in front of me. I understood that maybe people react the way they do because they don't know what to do– there was never an anti-David agenda. It was eye-opening to be on the other side.

Talking about stuttering with others was when I stopped feeling lonely and started feeling part of a group. Hearing "You are not alone" was nothing short of transformative. It felt like a weight was lifted off my shoulders. I had found my tr-tr-tr-tribe.

I had been attending our support meetings for a few months when a professor at the university invited us, the members of the NSA, to have a panel discussion about stuttering with her class. As a person who stutters, I had a paralyzing fear of public speaking, but Dr. Freeman challenged me to do it, and I reluctantly said yes.

The panel was hosted by Professor Jan Lougeay, who taught the stuttering class at the university. After the professor briefly introduced us, the students began asking us questions.

Do you know what words you will stutter on? Does anybody else in your family stutter? Do you stutter in your mind? Do you stutter in all languages? And so on.

It was the first time I was asked to "share my story" with others, and the students came prepared with insightful questions. It was both an introspective and enlightening experience as it forced me to look back and put into words the feelings I had growing up and my experiences leading up to that day. I was also fascinated by some of the answers from the other panelists. For starters, we all sounded vastly different. One of the panelists had many re-re-re-re-repetitions, while another would struggle mightily with the initial sound of a word but sounded pretty fluent after that initial block. Another one of the panelists didn't stutter at all (from what I could tell), but she said that she accomplished that by substituting words and going into tangents instead of just saying the first thing that came to her mind. She said she lived in fear of being "found out" and called herself a "covert stutterer."

My enduring memory of that day was that the professor and the students got a lot out of our stories. They were interested in what we had to say.

Over the past twelve years, I have been a dedicated participant in that stuttering class. For the first couple of years, I would sit at the back of the room, taking notes like my life depended on it; I wanted to know as much as I could about this thing called stuttering. Then, the professor started asking me questions when she thought I could clarify something for the students. After a few more years, I was practically doing a weekly joint-lecture with Professor Lougeay.

While I am not a speech pathologist, nor do I play one on the internet, living with a condition for over 30 years does make you a kind of expert. As time has passed, my involvement with the stuttering community has extended far beyond the confines of that classroom. I have been honored with invitations to serve as a panelist or lead discussions at universities in different countries. I have had the privilege of addressing elementary school students and parents of children who stutter. I have presented at conferences, facilitated in-person and online support groups, and contributed to numerous research projects. Along this journey, I've forged meaningful connections with numerous SLPs and have authored articles for national and international publications.

What I have learned over that time is that stuttering is still a big mystery. There is consensus about some details but debate about others. There are new publications and research projects every year, but we still don't have a cure. However, something Dr. Freeman told me years ago remained in my mind: the more we speak about it, the more we will understand this fascinating speech disorder.

With that in mind, one day, I started to document the questions we get asked the most during our panels, the ones people find more fascinating and some odd ones. This book you are holding is my best attempt at answering all of them. But as I learned at that first panel, stuttering is a very personal experience, and one person can't fully explain the wide variety of experiences and feelings that people who stutter live with daily. Because of that, apart from my answers, I have asked those same questions to hundreds of people who stutter from all over the world to give you the most expansive, in-depth view of stuttering possible.

Whether you are a person who stutters, a student, a practicing SLP, or a parent looking for answers, I hope this book helps you better understand stuttering.

One of our panels at the University of Texas at Dallas in 2019

Author's note: My very literal friend Aiden suggested that I tell you upfront that there are not exactly 1000 answers in this book. The number **1000** was a stylistic choice because it looks better as a title than a random number that ends in 61. We cool?

What is stuttering?

The National Institutes of Health defines stuttering as follows:

> Stuttering is a speech disorder characterized by repetition of sounds, syllables, or words; prolongation of sounds; and interruptions in speech known as blocks. An individual who stutters exactly knows what he or she would like to say but has trouble producing a normal flow of speech. These speech disruptions may be accompanied by struggle behaviors, such as rapid eye blinks or tremors of the lips. Stuttering can make it difficult to communicate with other people, which often affects a person's quality of life and interpersonal relationships. Stuttering can also negatively influence job performance and opportunities, and treatment can come at a high financial cost.
>
> Symptoms of stuttering can vary significantly throughout a person's day. In general, speaking before a group or talking on the telephone may make a person's stuttering more severe, while singing, reading, or speaking in unison may temporarily reduce stuttering.
>
> Stuttering is sometimes referred to as stammering and by a broader term, disfluent speech.

I think that is a good start; however, two critical things are missing from that definition: 1) The negative psychological impact that comes with the inability to speak your mind when and how you want, and 2) The great lengths some people who stutter (PWS) go to hide their stuttering, called **covert stuttering**.

Let's start with the psychological part.

For me, stuttering meant that something was broken in me. I don't remember the first moment I stuttered, but I imagine it being terrifying for a child. You think of something and know the words you want to say, but when you open your mouth…. Silence.

Except it's worse: You think of something and know the words you want to say, but when you try to open your mouth, your lips are stuck in place. You feel confused. You try again, opening your mouth effortlessly, but this time, your tongue is not moving like you want it to; it's trembling out of control. Seconds pass, and you are literally running out of air trying to make a sound. You notice that the listener looks confused but also like she is trying not to laugh. You look away, embarrassed that this keeps happening to you… and you still haven't said the first word.

This might happen with every word you try to say, with some or none of them; you never truly know what will happen until you open your mouth. Stuttering is highly variable and unpredictable.

Stuttering made me feel guilty when I noticed my parents and teachers worried about me. When somebody praises you for not stuttering, you internalize that stuttering is wrong and must be eliminated. Except most of the time I couldn't do that. I felt I was failing them, that I wasn't trying hard enough.

Losing control of your body is scary, and if it happens in front of somebody else, it's embarrassing. When it happens 50 times a day, every day, it starts affecting your behavior.

You might begin to use words different from the ones you genuinely want to say or choosing not to speak altogether. I had thoughts and ideas in my mind, but I knew I couldn't say them like I wanted to, so I kept them to myself. My stutter made me feel trapped. Many times, stuttering made a liar out of me when I knew the answer to a question but replied, "I don't know" instead.

In school, I didn't feel excluded, but I was more an observer than an active participant. Some kids would make jokes about me or give me offensive nicknames; I was bullied for something I had no control over. I often settled for a lower grade if that allowed me to skip reading out loud.

As I grew up, my stutter made me fear most speaking situations. Answering the phone? No, thank you. Asking for directions? I would rather get lost and find my way back. Asking a girl out? I'll just have imaginary conversations with myself and go to sleep feeling defeated for not trying when I had the opportunity. I mastered avoiding speaking situations, even if it meant missing out on things I truly wanted to do. My stutter made me feel that I had to dull my light.

Did I have *all* these feelings *all* the time? No. I thought of myself as a happy person. I had friends. I was good in school. My family loved me. I was confident in other areas. But one severe block was all I needed to push me into a downward spiral of negative feelings and go back into hiding. By telling you this, I do not intend to paint the bleakest picture of stuttering possible, but those are some of my real feelings growing up.

Since then, I have gone to speech therapy and counseling from a professional psychologist, both of which have made an enormous difference. I do public speaking for fun and have a healthy social life filled with conversations with great friends. I have a job I love, and I can speak multiple languages. I'm genuinely happy. Life is great!

… But I still stutter. I still can't say my name effortlessly. I still second-guess myself before opening my mouth. I still rehearse my order over and over before speaking to my server at a restaurant. Hearing my phone ring still makes my heart skip a beat. It bothers me way less, but it never truly goes away.

Now, let's talk about "covert stuttering."

Covert stuttering is when a person might not exhibit visible speech behaviors (repetitions, prolongations, or blocks) or be so subtle that a listener might not pick up on it. But this is only because the covert stutterer is constantly doing "mental gymnastics" like substituting words, speaking around trouble sounds, changing the speed of their speech, going on tangents, and generally doing whatever it takes not to be "discovered" as a person who stutters.

While a covert stutterer might pass as a "normal/fluent" speaker, on the inside, that person might be just as terrified of speaking as somebody who struggles to produce any sound. They may also be ashamed or embarrassed by all their effort to sound normal. They might have high levels of anxiety or low self-esteem, just like a person with more "overt" (noticeable) stuttering behaviors. It's exhausting.

I didn't know about covert stuttering until I became more active in the community. I thought that the more visible your symptoms were, the worse it would be, but over time, I realized that my assumptions were not necessarily accurate. The severity of the visible part of your stuttering (how often you repeat sounds, the length of your blocks, etc.) might not directly correlate with how much you feel your stuttering affects your life.

The topic of "severity" will be explored in-depth later in the book.

What causes stuttering?

The short answer is: we don't know yet. Researchers currently believe that stuttering is caused by a combination of factors, including genetics, language development, environment, and brain structure and function.

Most children will experience some dysfluencies[2] when they are young and learning to talk, but those are considered normal and will be outgrown as the child begins to master their speech and language skills. Only when those persist or become more pronounced and uncontrollable should you seek help for your child.

Everyone, adults included, can experience "stuttering" when they are nervous, surprised, or uncomfortable, but it's essential to differentiate those as normal dysfluencies and not the disorder formally known as stuttering.

Most people start stuttering during childhood when they are learning how to talk; however, there are other cases when stuttering develops in adulthood as the result of a brain injury or severe psychological trauma. Those cases are known as "acquired" or neurogenic stuttering, and they are caused by lesions to the language areas of the brain. Some of those cases can be overcome with speech therapy, but some might become permanent.

On the genetic side, researchers haven't pinpointed a specific gene to which stuttering can be attributed. Still, the fact that it can run in families indicates there is a genetic component to it.

---

[2] The prefix dys- is a combining form that means "bad," "abnormal," "impaired," or "difficult".

Roughly 1% of the population stutters. That is 80 million people worldwide and around 3 million people in the United States alone, but I imagine the actual number being higher since that number doesn't account for covert people.

Four out of five people who stutter are males. It is unclear why stuttering is more common in males, but it may be linked to genetic factors; females could be more resistant to inheriting a stutter or have better recovery rates than males.

It's important to note that stuttering is not a result of emotional or psychological problems, nor is it caused by a lack of intelligence. Those factors can worsen a stutter, but they are not the cause. Stuttering is no one's fault.

How is stuttering diagnosed?

Since most people who stutter start at an early age, the first step usually comes from the parents. If you notice your child stuttering, tensing when trying to talk, or beginning to avoid speaking situations, look for help. The earlier, the better. Professional help can be found by searching for a speech-language pathologist (SLP) or getting a referral from a nearby college offering speech disorder courses. SLPs work with many disorders, so try to find somebody with experience working with people who stutter.

An SLP diagnoses stuttering through a combination of methods. Some of them are:

Case History: Since stuttering can be genetic, it's essential to know if other family members have a history of stuttering. Having a family history of stuttering increases the possibility of having a stutter, but it's not a guarantee.

Observation and Assessment: The SLP will conduct an interview in which the individual's speech patterns are observed. This may include conversations, reading out loud, telling stories, or answering questions. The SLP will look for repetitions, blocks, prolongations, extended pauses, and secondary behaviors like facial contortions, unnatural body movements, or physical tension.

Speech evaluations: The SLP may conduct formal assessments to evaluate the individual's speech fluency rate, prosody, and overall communication skills. Standardized tests may measure the severity of stuttering (the number of dysfluencies per speech sample, for example) and its impact on daily communication.

Early intervention and appropriate treatment can significantly improve communication skills and quality of life for people who stutter.

It's important to note that stuttering can vary widely in severity and presentation, and the diagnostic process should be adapted accordingly to address each individual's unique needs.

In recent years, there has been a move from indicators like the number of dysfluencies per minute as the sole measure of severity to more holistic approaches that consider how much stuttering affects one's life on a personal level.

How do you measure "severity"?

This is a tricky one. Stuttering is characterized mainly by three behaviors: Repetitions, prolongations, and blocks. Every person who stutters has a unique combination of these behaviors. Generally speaking, re-re-repetitions are considered less severe than prooooollllllllloooooongations; and both of these are considered less severe than b------locks.

What I've learned over the past decade is that what you see is not everything there is. The blocks, repetitions, and physical signs of struggle are just a tiny part compared to everything that goes on in our minds before, during, and after stuttering. Your scale of severity depends on how much you struggle when you are trying to talk AND how much you let it affect you.

From a purely physiological standpoint, my stuttering is severe. I struggle with most of my words; it is ever-present. That said, I can confidently say that I don't care much about it at this point in my life. While I used to see my stutter as this defect that would ruin my chances of success and happiness, now I see it as a tiny part of me. It doesn't define who I am as a human. That is a massive change.

A common analogy in the stuttering community is "the stuttering iceberg," introduced by Joseph Sheehan in 1970. From the outside, it's impossible to know what's under the surface, so one cannot judge "severity" by just observing or listening to a person.

A stuttering iceberg could look like this:

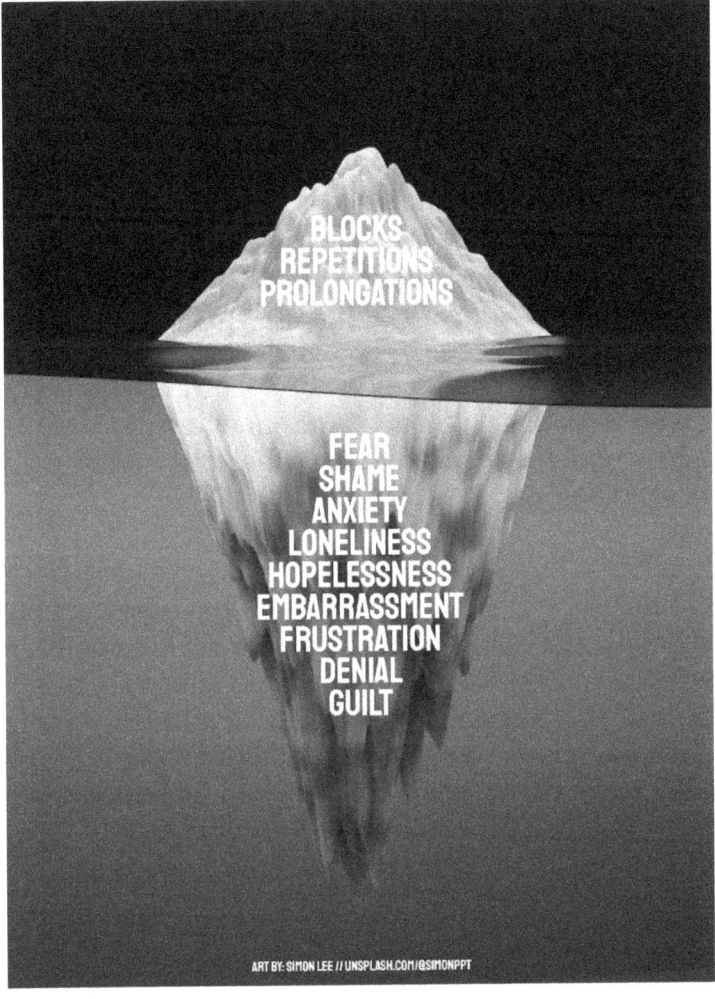

When I was younger, my physical struggle while speaking was severe, and my "below-the-surface" feelings were also very negative. I was perpetually afraid of opening my mouth, my anxiety before speaking was through the roof, and I felt generally embarrassed by my speech. I was unhappy being myself, and I thought my speech would forever impact my future. I was ashamed of talking like this.

Now, thanks to the help of my SLP and time, my physical struggle with speaking would still qualify as severe, but I have eliminated or transformed most of those "below-the-surface" negative feelings into positives. I have learned that while I still speak differently than others, it's not necessarily a negative if I get my message across and get to be part of the conversation. I have not only reluctantly accepted my speech as part of myself, but I have sometimes even embraced it as a positive! My iceberg might not look that different on the surface, but it's radically different under the surface, and that has made my life infinitely different.

This is not to say that my speech hasn't changed. Thanks to the help of my SLP and practice, I have learned many techniques that help increase my fluency, but fluency has stopped being my only goal. Now, I do public speaking for pleasure, tell stories, and dare to approach strangers (sometimes, I still struggle with this one), but the fact that I stutter while doing those activities has little impact on my well-being.

Does everyone stutter the same?

No. Within the stuttering world, we use the expression, "The only consistent thing about stuttering is that it is inconsistent." Differences exist from person to person and from one situation to the next.

My stuttering has evolved and gone through phases as I have grown up. My mother said that the first time she noticed me stuttering, it was like I "couldn't get my voice going." Eventually, she saw that I needed more effort to say things. I started jumping in place or clenching my fists to push sounds out. She doesn't remember me doing many repetitions while talking, and my stuttering these days is still characterized more by long, silent blocks than anything else.

As you go through life, sometimes you stumble upon an action that helps you get a word out, and those behaviors become tricks you repeat, called "secondary behaviors." Some of the things I have used over the years are tapping a foot while talking, secretly pinching myself before saying a word, biting my tongue trying to release a particularly severe block, waving my hands like an orchestra director while on the phone, closing my eyes while talking and many, many, MANY more.

Lee Reeves, founder of the Dallas chapter of the National Stuttering Association, likes to say, "If you have met one person who stutters, you have met one person who stutters," meaning you shouldn't assume that what you see in one person who stutters will necessarily be present in others. This variability is what makes stuttering so challenging to treat.

When and how did you first realize that you stutter?

I don't remember exactly when I noticed it, but the first time I remember it being an issue was during a spelling bee in first grade. The whole class was standing up, and we went around the classroom spelling words. If you got it wrong, you had to sit down, and the last person standing was the winner. We went around the room several times, and people were getting eliminated as words got harder. Around ten people were standing when my turn to speak again came. My word was "violin," a word I knew how to spell… but as I opened my mouth, I couldn't get the letters out! Feeling confused, I struggled for a few seconds until the teacher finally told me to sit down. I was out. I sat with my head down, feeling angry, frustrated, and wronged.

I think most of my early stuttering memories are school-related and very similar to other people's: having difficulty saying my name, anxiety about reading out loud in front of others, embarrassment and frustration when you can't answer a question you know the answer to, trying to find ways to get out of the classroom to avoid talking, kids mocking me and giving me nicknames, etc.

Stuttering is rarely well received by the people around you, immediately making you aware that something is "wrong" with you. This is how the negative underside of the iceberg begins to form.

Before I went to school, the neighbor kids used to call me stutterbug. Then, in first grade, I was placed in the slow readers group because they thought I didn't know the words. - Larry B. (Pittsburgh, PA)

Third grade at recess, waiting in line to play tetherball. When I opened my mouth, I couldn't talk normally anymore. I was in a state of shock. - Josh V. (Stockton, CA)

In kindergarten, another student pointed it out and teased me. My grandmother and uncle stuttered, so until then, it felt normal to me. - Bobby G. (Massachusetts)

Six years old. I noticed the reaction of my teachers… they seemed concerned. - Tyrone R. (South Africa)

I don't know when I started, but I noticed it at eleven years old when family and friends would say, 'Spit it out!' That's when I realized I spoke differently. - Jessica J. (Ohio)

When one of my teachers asked me to get up to read, I started shaking my whole body to get the words out. - Pedro A. (Portugal)

I raised my hand to answer in French class but couldn't speak. I was 12. I may have had some kind of stroke that affected my speech at that moment. It was as sudden as that. From one second to another, my life changed. - Rachel A. (London, UK)

When I woke up from a coma after a terrible car accident. I had never stuttered before that. - Sheree M. (Gladstone, Queensland)

In elementary school. I was seen as the shy kid because I tried hiding my stuttering by not talking. - Karina L. (Los Angeles, CA)

How would you explain stuttering to others based on your personal experience?

I usually explain it as a "short circuit" or miscommunication between my brain and the rest of the system (lungs, jaw, tongue, various muscles, etc) used to create speech. I don't stutter in my mind, so my thoughts are fluent and cohesive, or as much as that can be said about anybody, but when I try to say my thoughts aloud, the sounds just don't come out like I want them to or when I want them to. Sometimes, the disruption can be with the first sound I'm trying to make; other times, my speech is perfectly fluent for a few words before the disruptions start again. Sometimes I feel blocked even before I try to make the first sound; it's very unpredictable!

I like the following analogy:

> *Stuttering is like having a knee joint that lets you fold your leg in all directions instead of just backward. Every time you step and put weight on it, you can't predict how you will lean in, so you are always scared of falling.* - Hakim A. (Algeria)

That feeling of not being in control is very overwhelming. It causes you to second-guess yourself every time you open your mouth and ultimately forces you (depending on your severity level and other factors) not even to try to speak.

I usually explain it as a delay between your brain and voice cords. - Katrina L. (Rock Hill, SC)

It is like sending something to print, and it takes forever to get printed out because of an undetermined connection issue. - Frank R. (Miami, FLA)

It is a neurological disorder (like Tourettes). There's nothing wrong with my mouth or my throat or anything related to my speech apparatus. - Mike B (Coventry, UK)

For me, it feels like my brain knows a song's melody and words, but when my mouth tries to play it, it skips and gets stuck like a scratched CD. - Maggie D. (Pittsburgh, PA)

It's like pushing a rock uphill with your face. Exhausting. - Jason S. (Mankato, MN)

I want to talk way faster than my brain can process properly. - Kiyanna W. (Middletown, OH)

What is the most common feeling you associate with stuttering?

In my younger days, I would've said loneliness, frustration, anger, embarrassment, and shame. I felt I couldn't be myself around other people because every time I opened my mouth, I didn't have the certainty that my words would come out. I had anxiety before every speaking situation. Embarrassment, confusion, and frustration during the moments of stuttering. Shame after.

As I grew up, I felt hopeless. I knew I was smart, but it was tough to show it to people because I couldn't talk "normally." I constantly felt judged unfairly.

Stuttering can be very damaging to our mental health, and for most of us, it is mostly invisible. Carl Jung's quote from the book *Memories, Dreams, Reflections sums it up:* "Loneliness does not come from having no people around one, but from being unable to communicate the things that seem important to oneself."

> *For sure, frustration. I can't even explain what we go through daily to someone who has no idea. I would also add sadness and embarrassment. - Lance L. (Ft. Worth, TX)*
>
> *Anxiety, embarrassment, frustration, depression. - Elisha S. (Trinidad)*
>
> *Embarrassed, misunderstood, insulted, forgotten, left behind, regret. - Samantha B. (Petal, MS)*

> *Anger: when I was in school, I knew the answers but couldn't speak up. Also, depression and loneliness. - Munir E. (Las Vegas, NV)*
>
> *Frustration, anger, anxiety, and depression. - Sean J. (Ottawa, ON)*
>
> *Embarrassment, frustration, anger, and a feeling of 'being less than' all wrapped into one. - Carl M. (Newark, AR)*
>
> *Suffocation, loneliness, heartbreak. - Gasem A. (Jordan)*

On the flip side, all those feelings have changed dramatically as I have grown up, matured, received help from a therapist, and found the support of a community. Finding out that people wanted to hear what I had to say, despite my stuttering and precisely because of it, dramatically transformed my perception of myself. Discovering I was not alone and that there was a worldwide community of people who stutter was liberating.

Today, the feelings I associate with stuttering are love (my ex-girlfriend stutters), belonging, empathy, growth, resilience, and purpose.

Time, maturity, and talking to others have made me see stuttering not as one definite thing but as something with many shades and levels, an evolving thing. Nowadays, stuttering is such a big part of my life in a positive way that I can say I'm proud to stutter and mean it.[3]

---

[3] Somebody show that to my twelve-year-old self!

What would you want other people to understand about stuttering?

One of the most important things to know is that stuttering is a complex disorder that still confuses researchers, therapists, and people who stutter alike. Stuttering is a neurological disorder not caused by my nervousness or fear; it's just how I speak. I don't know why I do it. I would also like people to be more patient. We live in a fast-paced world; most people listen only to reply, not to understand your words. Being impatient can be hard on people with trouble communicating "normally." Being patient, kind, and understanding goes a long way with people who stutter.

> *I would like people to realize that there is a difference between tripping over words because you're talking too fast and a diagnosed speech disorder. Something to know about my speech is that my severity is on a sliding scale. It depends on my mood, how much sleep I get, who I talk to, etc. If I seem fluent one day, don't be fooled; it didn't just disappear. - Michelle D. (New York)*
>
> *I don't stutter intentionally or for attention, and it hurts when they laugh at me. I'm not dumb. - Carol B. (Texas)*
>
> *That having a stutter does not indicate other personality traits. People who stutter can be effective communicators - politicians, speakers, actors, debaters - even when openly stuttering. - Jade H. (Portland, OR)*

Every single day is a struggle, and it's exhausting. We all try and put on a brave face, but deep down, we are very frustrated - Jason S. (Minnesota)

That I can't just "slow down and think about what I'm going to say." - Bryan C. (Connecticut)

That stuttering has nothing to do with a lack of confidence, insecurity, low self-esteem, nervousness, or shyness. If people who stutter have any of those characteristics, this has nothing to do with their disfluencies but how others perceive and treat them. People who stutter can be great teachers, great leaders, great doctors, great professors, great lawyers, great nurses, and a lot more. - Mark W. (The Netherlands)

What are common misconceptions about stuttering?

People think I stutter because I'm nervous. While feeling nervous can affect my fluency, I usually stutter, nervous or not. I can have the best day of my life but still struggle to say my name. My feelings affect it, but they are not the cause. Telling me to relax doesn't help.

You can overcome it if you try hard enough. I guarantee you I think about my speech more than 98% of the people. If it depended on effort alone, I would not stutter. I have tried therapy, drugs, singing, meditation, reading out loud, praying, learning different languages, hypnosis, home remedies, and wishing really, really hard that it goes away while I blow out the candles on my birthday cake... but I still stutter. It's not that I don't try hard enough; it's just how I talk.

It's related to intelligence. While I can't generalize about the relationship between IQ and stuttering, I can tell you that some people treat you like you are dumb when you can't speak normally. I've had people talk to me eeeennnnuuuuunciaaaaaatiiiing reaaaaaally slooooowly and making uncomfortable eye contact like that is going to make me stutter less. I've had people try to speak to me in Spanish (which they clearly don't speak) because they assume my stuttering comes from not knowing English. I've had people walk away when I take too long to say a word. Stuttering is just how I talk; it doesn't relate much to other skills, abilities, or intelligence.

Have you tried singing? Yes. Unfortunately, this isn't *High School Musical,* and singing every word through life is not a sustainable strategy. When we sing, we use different parts of our brain, and that's why a large number of people who stutter don't stutter when singing. However, physiologically speaking, they are two different processes, and singing won't cure my stuttering. That being said, it is definitely a fun party trick! Starting to rap in front of somebody and seeing their jaws drop is still one of my top 5 things to do after a few drinks... but again, it's not a cure.

My (insert relative) used to stutter, and once he (insert activity), he stopped stuttering. Stuttering is a complex disorder; what worked for one person might not work for anybody else. Some kids outgrow it, but that might mean they had normal disfluencies while learning to talk, not the communication disorder known as stuttering. With the help of therapy and practice, you can learn some level of control, but how proficient and automatic your speech becomes after that will depend on factors like your age, your environment, and even your genes. There is no one-size-fits-all.

What was it like in school?

In elementary school, I typically got good grades without trying too hard. I was a good student. That being said, avoiding speaking situations became an art. I would find creative ways to avoid answering questions, getting out of participating in class, or reading out loud. I avoided it so much that stuttering wasn't much of an issue on a day-to-day basis, but it was always on my mind. Before any activity that involved speaking, I remember feeling anxious and dreaded.

When I was about to start middle school, my family had financial problems, and we had to move to a smaller town. My new school was very different than the one I had attended before. There, I was met by three kids who seemed to have a thing against me, and they made it a habit of bullying me. Sometimes, it was because of my speech, but other times, it felt like they didn't even need a reason to do it; they just enjoyed it. I only attended that school for one year, but it was a difficult one. The difficulties weren't 100% related to my stuttering— it was a challenging year for everybody in my family, but I remember that year making me VERY self-conscious about being different. My stutter and my feelings about it got significantly worse that year.

Luckily, there was a silver lining to that horrible school year: I became good friends with the girl who sat beside me every day. Her name was Haydée, and like me, she was new to the school. I don't know who started it, but throughout the day, we would pass notes talking about our day, making each other laugh, asking questions about the class, etc.

That year, I discovered the power of writing as a means of self-expression. Being able to communicate with her without talking made me feel unshackled. In writing, I could tell stories, use my whole vocabulary without fear, and ask whatever came to mind. Being bullied at recess didn't suck as much when I could talk to her in the next class. During that problematic year, her friendship made a considerable difference, and we remain friends.

My family moved again the following year, and the school I started attending was smaller. Bullying wasn't much of an issue, but as I was growing older, presentations in class were more of a thing, and I struggled terribly with them. Here, some teachers let me have the option of not doing presentations in class, and at the time, that felt like a huge help, but looking back, I think their kindness just made me even more comfortable with avoiding speaking situations. Now, I believe it would've been better if the teachers pushed me a little outside of my comfort zone.

During middle and high school, I also started to get more interested in girls, and I remember feeling that my stutter was a big wall between me and them (except for Haydée). With the benefit of hindsight, I can admit that it was less that girls were rejecting me and more me being too scared to talk to them, but I still felt that I was struggling more than my peers. I felt lonely.

My college experience was generally positive. I liked going to school and the projects I was working on, but I remember feeling a general anxiety about growing older and getting a job.

Even though I felt I had the skills to succeed, I was starting to realize how stuttering would make even mundane tasks harder. When you start having to take care of your own paperwork and bureaucratic procedures, speaking and advocating for yourself becomes more of an everyday task. Stuttering can genuinely be an obstacle in those scenarios.

> *I kept my speaking to a minimum in middle/high school. When I stuttered, I was laughed at or got funny looks. I tried to hide it, downplay it, and convince myself it wasn't an issue (wrong move), so I ended up not seeking speech therapy until I was well into college. Things got a lot better after high school. A few good memories aside, I doubt I'll ever be nostalgic for that time because a good deal of what I remember is sitting there, palms sweating, nervously anticipating the next time I would have to talk. - Michael H. (Lufkin, TX)*
>
> *I hid it and still do to this day. I'm still working on letting myself stutter. I would find synonyms all day before allowing myself to stutter in front of anybody. - Gretchen M. (Duluth, MN)*
>
> *I was lucky to have many friends, so I never got bullied. I used to hate having to read out loud in English classes. The teacher used to go from row to row, and I can, to this day, remember my palms getting sweaty and my heart rate going up as it got closer to me. Horrible experience. - James N. (Ireland)*
>
> *I hated high school; the teasing was unbearable. I even had a teacher tell me I should not have speaking jobs and go into journalism or factory work so I wouldn't have to talk. - Gary A. (Chicago, IL)*

I had speech therapy through the school system until 4th grade. I felt singled out, but making fun of me didn't occur until I had to transfer from a small private all-girls school to a large public high school. There, teachers didn't directly address the laughing in the room when I gave a speech or had to read out loud. It greatly added to my anxiety. College and pharmacy school were very stressful. I saw my anxiety skyrocket, and I didn't directly address my stuttering. I would've had a much more positive college experience if I had known to do so. - Rebecca M. (Huntsville, AL)

In elementary school, most kids didn't care that I stuttered. There was a bit of teasing here and there, but teachers were quick to shut it down. I would get in trouble for talking too much. In 8th grade, I stuttered, and the whole class laughed, including the teacher. I started hiding it after that until I was about 19. - Brianna P. (Dallas, TX)

I fought every day with those who tried to tease or bully me. Ignorant classmates thought I was dumb because I stuttered. I had no friends because I didn't talk to anyone, and no one ever spoke to me. Luckily, in high school, they had a program where you could work to earn credit for graduation outside a traditional classroom while picking up valuable skills and trades. That saved me from dropping out. - Anthony D. (San Diego, CA)

My speech didn't become a serious issue until I began college and graduate school. At this point, I was pretty severe and dealt with several male professors who saw me as an easy target. I experienced the most heinous and sadistic behavior in these years. Add that I didn't understand stuttering, know my rights, or could even fathom living with it. I didn't know how. I was alone. I don't know how I did it. These were some of the most desperate times in my life. Absolute grotesque abuse. - Amey H. (Indiana)

Fortunately, I had good experiences in school. My teachers and classmates were very supportive. I got some accommodations, but they also encouraged me to expand my comfort zone and do exciting things. In high school, I was the cool guy who played in several bands and who taught his classmates drumming. My musical skills were much more important than the way I spoke. I felt valued and learned at a very young age that my stuttering was only a part of me and that I had many other qualities. In the Netherlands we only have public schools, but we have a lot of different school systems. We have Montessori, Jena Plan, and Anthroposophical schools. I went to an Anthroposophical School, like my whole family. In this education approach, they teach cognitive, emotional, creative, and social skills. Children are taught to care for each other, treat each other with respect, and that everyone is different and has individual qualities. Bullying or excluding other children was and is not allowed in any way. - Mark W. (The Netherlands)

I just talked to very few people and lived in my headphones. I hated people's reactions to my speech and was full of anger. - Shannon C. (Canada)

How do you handle your stuttering when meeting people for the first time?

Allow me to repeat myself: introductions suck! Most people who stutter report having trouble saying their names. There are probably many reasons for this, but I think it's because our name is a word we can't substitute or talk around, together with the fact that we have failed on it so many times before that we are anxious about having to go through that again.

During introductions, most people expect you to say your name within seconds. Unfortunately, when you struggle to say it, you get what we, people who stutter, call "the look," which is a mix of confusion/judgment on the face of your listener.

Now that I am older, I don't let it affect me too much, but when I was younger, "the look" made me hesitant to talk to people. Just imagine how you would feel if every time you opened your mouth, you saw the expression on the listener's change to a mix of confusion, concern, and even laughter. It can be devastating for someone's self-esteem.

Then, if the introduction comes with a handshake, you add a new level of awkwardness to the whole interaction. Think about it: what do you do when you are holding someone's hand but can't say your name for 5-10 seconds? Do you keep shaking hands until you get the words out? Do you stop shaking but keep holding the hand? Do you let go and hope they don't move on before you say your name?
It might sound inconsequential, but when you stutter, these little things cause most introductions to start with the wrong foot.

I have introduced myself with a different name a hundred times. Not because I forgot mine (like people like to ask jokingly[4]), but because as a person who stutters, sometimes you have to pick your battles, and if you think you won't see this person again, who cares if you change it to something easier to say, right? Except sometimes, that backfires.

Some years ago, my friend Mark and I started to play pool on Thursday nights. The first night, we got a table and started playing standard stuff. An hour in, a couple of guys approached our table and asked if we would want to play 2v2. Mark, probably tired of kicking my ass, said yes. When we were about to start playing, the other guys did the usual thing and introduced themselves. When my turn came, I couldn't get my name out, so without thinking, I just blurted out the first name that came to mind: "John!" I don't think Mark noticed, but I thought, "Who cares? I won't see these guys again."

We played a few more games, had a few more beers, and ended the night. Fun times.

Fast forward one week, we go to the same spot again, and as soon as we walk through the door, I hear a voice coming from the back of the room, "John, my man! How is it going?!"

DAMMIT!!

---

[4] Don't be one of them, please, it's not funny.

This time, I remember Mark turning to me and asking, "Who the hell is John?" So, I had to explain that I had said a different name the previous week because of my stutter, which he found amusing. As we walked to the pool tables, I had a mental debate: Should I continue being John or try to introduce myself as David and explain what happened last week? It was too much, so I ended up being John. Again. This probably happened 10 years ago, but I still remember it because I felt like a liar whenever I responded to my fake name. I was letting my stutter control my actions.

I'm not going to lie to you and say that introductions have gotten easier; they suck, and they still do, but my approach to them is very different. I now have a joke or two ready when I am introducing myself. Something like "Wait for it… it will be worth it" or "Give me a second, I'm buffering." Followed by a quick explanation of what stuttering is. I feel it's the best way to break the ice and bring attention to my stuttering more positively (I own it; it's not that serious, relax!), and the results have been infinitely more positive. Most people are more patient and understanding once you explain that you have a condition you can't control.

People's reactions are usually a reflection of how you portray yourself. I stutter severely, but I love talking and try to present myself as somebody worth listening to. I try to speak confidently, and that commands respect because people see that words don't come easy.

That said, I only became this guy in my early thirties. It took me years of missing chances and hating meeting new people to realize that the first person I had to convince that my words were important was myself. I promise that the sooner you get there, the better your life will be.

Finally, I am obligated to say that now and then, I still say a different name, but only on specific occasions. Let's say I'm at a Starbucks in a different city, there are too many people behind me, I am in a rush... I can be John for five seconds. I don't recommend avoidance behaviors to anybody, but sometimes, you must pick your battles.

> *I always struggle with anxiety when meeting adults since I've had so many bad reactions before. The anxiety definitely makes my stutter worse. My stutter usually makes it difficult to say my name, which is embarrassing (people have jokingly asked if I've forgotten it many times). I've also noticed that others interrupt and talk over me if I start stuttering. I see they look away or feel uncomfortable. It's tough to make friends as an adult. - Alyssa N. (Herriman, Utah)*
>
> *I bring up my stuttering in a subtle way. Usually, I say a quick, 'That was a good one' after I stutter, and then I tell them I stutter. I get that business out of the way ASAP. - Amey H. (Indiana)*
>
> *I always try to fit it in the first greeting. A small joke like 'If you wonder, I don't have lag; I just stutter' (I have many gamer friends). If I introduce the subject, I can control the conversation, and if I start with a joke, I can show that I don't take it seriously, and neither should they. - Jochem S. (Netherlands)*

Did you ever believe that "it would just go away," and when it didn't, how did you cope?

Growing up, I constantly dreamed of waking up one day, and my stuttering would be gone. As time went by and it didn't "cure itself," I remember feeling hopeless. I don't know how I coped with it; I just continued my life and did my best. I didn't accept myself; it was more resignation.

Every time somebody mentioned a "cure," I would get a spark of excitement, but I soon realized that most advice came down to "relax," "breathe," "think before you speak," or "you should read out loud". None of those worked for me or were particularly insightful.

When I first started to go to speech therapy at around 28 years old, my speech pathologist told me that what I had was called stuttering and that I could learn to control it to some extent, but more than likely, it was going to be part of my life forever. In some way, that was one of the best things to hear because it removed all those false hopes of a miracle cure. It put me on a journey of acceptance that helped me turn my life around. I started working more on my mindset than on my actual speech, which impacted my life more than anything else I had done up to that point.

I still believe that accepting who you are is the first step in improving your life. Playing the cards you are dealt will always be better than hoping for new ones.

It got better when I accepted it. If I accept that I am a stutterer, I can change how I feel about it. The more I talk, the more confidence I have. The more confidence, the less I stutter. More confidence is not a cure, but I am a retail manager today, and I do not let my stutter stop me. My choices are to accept it and live life or not to accept it and hide. - Jason M. (Louisville, KY)

As I am now 62 years old, I look upon my stammer this way: It ain't going to disappear; it's a part of me, and I have to accept it. All I can do is be comfortable with it. If all I have to contend with in life is a stammer, it ain't that bad. There are a helluvah lot of people living with conditions they can't do much about. A lot of the stigma behind stammering is judgment. This can be done by whoever you are speaking to or by yourself. This is when the emotions kick in: the underbelly, the lack of self-esteem, and the feeling of being inferior to others. If you're happy to stutter without negative thoughts about how you speak, you're in a good place. It's not easy to cancel out old ingrained behaviors and bring a new way to speak into your life, but at least you can give it a go. - Mark M. (England)

Was there a pivotal moment that changed how you viewed stuttering?

I grew up in Mexico, and even though my family tried everything to help me, there were no stuttering specialists around me. The first time I visited a speech pathologist, I was already in my late twenties. It differed from all my previous experiences in that she didn't call it something it wasn't. She didn't say it was anxiety. She didn't say it would disappear with medication. She said in plain language, "You have what we call stuttering, and this is what we know about it." That was very refreshing. I felt that it finally gave me a precise diagnosis, and even though it also took away some of the hope I had for a miracle cure, in the long run, it was the best for me because it gave me an understanding of what stuttering was. Demystifying stuttering was the start of my journey of acceptance; I felt it lifted something off of my shoulders.

Another one of those moments came when I was around 27 years old. I was hanging out with friends late at night, and we walked into a local pizza spot to get a slice. When it came time for me to order, I stuttered, but the girl at the counter smiled the whole time. When I finished speaking, she said, "*Talking to you is fun; I felt like every word had a cliffhanger!*" That has always stuck with me because it was maybe the first time a girl said she liked talking to me BECAUSE of my stutter. She saw the silver lining, and it opened the door to consider a positive aspect of my stuttering.

Another big one was when, thanks to the suggestion of my speech pathologist, I joined an organization called Toastmasters. In this group, you can practice giving speeches and learn leadership skills. The idea of joining a public speaking group sounded terrifying, but my SLP said it could be beneficial. My first meetings were as scary as I imagined. Getting in front of my club and speaking would fill me with anxiety and leave me a sweaty mess, but over time, it got easier, and I started to realize that some of my assumptions about speaking were just wrong. Hearing everybody in the group talk about their fear (terror!) of speaking in public made me realize that I spoke differently, but the fear of being judged was universal. Over time, I even entered contests, winning many of them. I have continued attending the club for over a decade and honestly love public speaking now. Toastmasters played a big part in this.

Finally, my first conference of the National Stuttering Association was also a massive turning point. Getting there and realizing that I was surrounded by close to 900 people who spoke like me shattered all those ideas I previously had about being alone. Walking down the hotel halls and hearing stuttering all around me felt like an alternate reality— a welcoming, love-filled reality. Attending workshops and talks led by people who stutter opened my eyes to what was possible. I always assumed nobody would have the patience to sit and hear me speak for more than a minute, but there I was, listening to hours of people stuttering, and they all sounded intelligent and confident.

If that wasn't enough, the keynote speaker at that conference was David Seidler (RIP), the award-winning screenwriter for The King's Speech, just months from his victorious night at the 2011 Oscars.

David also grew up feeling that stuttering would stop him from achieving great things, yet there he was, telling us how he had reached the top of his profession precisely because of his stuttering when he wrote the story of King George VI of England.

His speech was fantastic and inspirational, but two quotes resonated with me that evening, and I must share them with you. The first one is:

"If you can live through a childhood of stuttering, you can live through anything. You have been tempered by the fire."

This quote made me feel that whatever I had experienced because of my stutter had a purpose. Hearing those words didn't change my past, but it made me think that I could use all those bad or negative experiences as fuel to move forward. I was already getting there thanks to the help of my SLP, but hearing David, a fellow stutterer, cemented the idea in my mind.

The second one is the definition of acceptance as a person who stutters. David related to us how one night, as a teenager, he was in his room, frustrated by his speech, angry with life, when in a chaotic outburst of emotion, he told himself:

"If I'm stuck with stuttering, f*** the rest of you, you are stuck listening to me!"

David was tired of hiding and feeling shame for being who he was. He was done being silent.

Those words meant the world to me. My first conference with the NSA was one of the most influential weekends of my life.

When I went to a speech therapist after having no therapy for over 28 years, I learned that stuttering was not my fault. I also learned about the NSA and found many Facebook groups. Since then, I have been on a journey to love and accept myself, stutter and all. - Lisa G. (Brockton, MA)

Acting on stage with a stutter was pretty cool. The first two nights were pretty good, but the last night, I did my monologue with complete fluency, and I am glad I can say that I acted on stage and didn't let my fear win. - Jairus W. (Atlanta, GA)

The first time I went to a stuttering conference, a guy got up to give a presentation and stuttered big-time, yet he gave a good presentation, and everybody applauded. I thought, "Hell, I can do that." My life hasn't been the same since. - James M. (Albuquerque, NM)

I simply got tired of being a victim and feeling like my "true self" was trapped inside of me. I got tired of my stutter having all the control, like I was a puppet on a string. So, I did the scariest thing and started an Instagram page where I make videos on various stuttering topics. I can honestly say that accepting my stutter and getting out of my comfort zone was the best thing I ever did. - Rhiannon S. (Waxahachie, TX)

A pivotal moment for me was when a dear friend advised me to 'just stutter' when I was nervous about speaking at an event, and that's when I learned to stop fighting my stutter. It no longer defines who I am, which has helped me become more fluent. - Sandy A. (Oklahoma City)

When my speech therapist asked me why I was apologizing for stuttering. – Jennifer R. (Philadelphia, PA)

I have two. The first was when I did an excellent presentation in front of my class, and everyone told me at the end how good I did. I finally felt like I was a part of the class. My second one was after attending my first NSA conference. I realized I wasn't alone and had the biggest support system ever!! - Michele D. (Buffalo, NY)

In my grade 10 year, I changed schools and told my new classmates that I stuttered. I realized that this is who I am, and I had to live my life to the fullest - Grace L. (Halifax, Nova Scotia)

David Seidler speaking at the NSA Conference in 2011

What advice would you give to individuals who struggle to accept themselves?

My friend Lee Reeves once shared how his speech therapist exemplified the point of stuttering being just a tiny part of him by drawing this on a piece of paper:

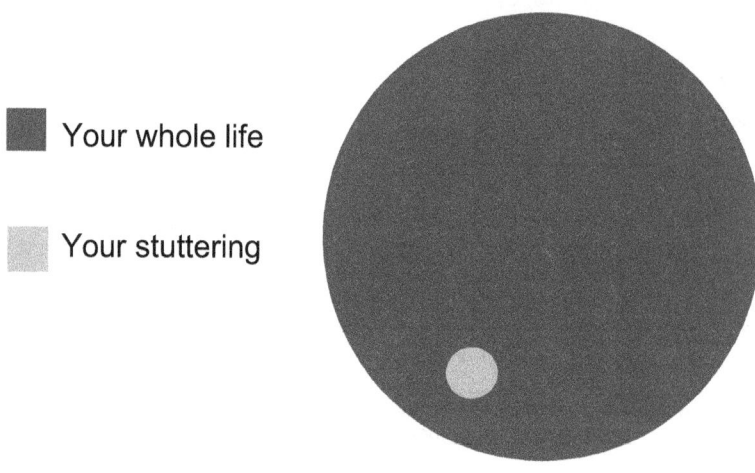

I had a similar realization in my late twenties when my speech therapist told me that talking was not the only activity that defined who I was. As a person who stutters, it's tough to accept that as truth, but once I took inventory of my life, I realized that I was good at many other things, and stuttering began to weigh less on my mind. I knew that people thought I was funny and liked being around me. I was a talented artist, and people respected that. I also started writing more and understood that there are many ways to communicate.

Stuttering seems less of a burden if you excel at other things, so start working on yourself! Work out (a healthy mind in a healthy body), educate yourself, become interesting, learn new skills, help others, be valuable, and be nice to people. The more you put yourself out there, the more examples you will find of people not caring about your speech. It sounds cliché, but your stuttering is an impediment only if you think it is.

Also, find help and support. That can be speech therapy, a support group for people who stutter, a good group of friends that will uplift you when you are down, or a combination. Nobody can do everything alone; having a solid community around you will make all the difference.

When I started attending meetings of the National Stuttering Association, one of the first realizations I had was how little I ever talked about stuttering with anybody throughout my life. Feeling that nobody understood what I was going through, I kept these experiences to myself. By my 20s, I had hundreds of experiences that I never shared with anybody. These memories made me feel like an outcast and contributed to my feelings of shame.

As time passed and I became a regular at these meetings, I could listen to other people's experiences and share my own, making me feel understood, validated, and less lonely. I was now part of a community.

The power of "the talking cure" is well documented. In his book *Why We Remember*, Charan Ranganath, PhD, says, *"The transformative effect of social interactions on life narratives might be the 'special sauce' that explains the efficacy of so many forms of psychotherapy, whether one-on-one or in group settings."*

Showing up to a support meeting can be intimidating, but now we have options to do so from the comfort of our homes. I would recommend joining *Stutter Social* (www.stuttersocial.com), searching for groups on Facebook ("Stuttering Community" is the biggest one in English), and getting connected— There's no reason to be alone anymore.

> *I encourage the person to connect with others in the stuttering community and understand that everyone is in a different place in their journey with stuttering. I highly recommend looking for role models in the stuttering community, reflecting on why you admire that person, and trying to emulate them. I would also discuss how we can foster self-compassion since we need to be kind to ourselves and be supportive of other people. Self-compassion is linked with self-acceptance. - Lisa N. (China)*
>
> *You can be so very much and express yourself in so many ways; why let your speech hold you back? Acceptance doesn't happen suddenly for most; it takes years to find it, but realizing that no one is perfect helps. - Stephanie C. (Plum, PA)*

Acceptance is a long and dynamic road! It's important to let yourself feel frustrated and disappointed - those feelings are normal and shouldn't be ignored. At the same time, acceptance is an achievable practice. A big part of acceptance for me was finding professional help that integrated speech therapy and emotional therapy. Stuttering in front of people and believing my words are worth the wait is an everyday challenge I choose to confront! It's tiring - so having support is vital. You can do it! - Nora S. (Milwaukee, WI)

What you resist will persist. - Muhammad A. (South Africa)

You are important because this is how God/higher power made you. You can accept yourself, stuttering and all, because you were wonderfully and masterfully made, handpicked by God. Others accept you and love you for who you are, stuttering and all! Surround yourself with those people and openly receive and accept their love. Lastly, be gentle with yourself. Your stutter is a part of you but does not define you and is not a flaw. When struggling in a moment of stuttering, stay as present as possible, attune to your body/thoughts/emotions, and focus on the conversation and the person, not how you say something. It's tough, I know, but it's possible with practice and kindness with yourself. Go slow. Keep practicing self-care, self-love, and relaxation. You are WORTH IT!!! - Christine D. (Indiana)

What advice would you give to a parent of a child who stutters?

First, be patient with your child and ensure they feel accepted and loved. Before talking about therapy or support groups, showing that you love them no matter what has to be the number one priority. I was lucky that my family was always very supportive and that they pushed me to not give up on my dreams. Even though I was struggling and felt "different," I always knew they had my back, which, unfortunately, is not always the case for everybody.

When I asked my parents about this, they shared that they felt guilty and alone throughout my childhood. **Know that it's not your fault.** You didn't cause it. Even if you are a person who stutters yourself and feel it's your fault that your child stutters, it's not your fault.

And you are not alone either. Find an SLP (speech-language pathologist in the US) with stuttering experience. Not every SLP is the same, and finding someone with experience and interest in stuttering can make a huge difference, especially if you start early. Early intervention is the number one determinant of success in therapy, but always pay attention to what the kid thinks and feels about treatment. Are they enjoying it? Is it helping? Some children don't want therapy, are not ready to put in the necessary work to make a difference, or the particular therapy setting is not suitable for them. Pay attention and know that therapy might not be what the child wants today, but they might reconsider and want to do it at another time. Put the option on the table and be supportive of their decision.

A couple of years ago, I attended a presentation by Dr. Courtney Byrd, director of the *Blank Center for Stuttering Education and Research* in Austin. She gave a beautiful presentation about talking to your children about stuttering openly. She said that making stuttering a taboo topic creates a "conspiracy of shame," and I couldn't agree more. Ask your child about their feelings, and treat their stuttering as something you all care about, which can be discussed openly. Talking about it might not cure it, but it helps prevent building the negative side of your child's "stuttering iceberg."

Aside from therapy, I am a big advocate of support groups. Growing up, I never met another kid who stuttered, so I always felt alone and misunderstood. Through my involvement with the NSA and other organizations, I have seen that children who grow up with the support of others are way better adjusted and comfortable in their skin. This is because they know others who "get them" and that what they feel is not unique. I've said it before, but finding "your tribe" is life-changing.

Luckily, we are now in the middle of a boom of support groups for stuttering, and finding one is just a search away.

Also –and this WILL NOT be everybody's cup of tea— my family is generally hilarious, and when we tease each other, they never treat my stuttering as off-limits. I appreciated that very much in some ways because it made it seem normal and just part of me. **I firmly believe nobody can hurt you if you can laugh at your stuttering.**

Let them know that improvement can be achieved from two ends: gaining more speech control (stuttering more easily or fluency) and learning to minimize negative views of stuttering. The iceberg analogy can be talked about and start melting it on both ends. - Mitchell Trichon, PhD (New York)

If you can help your child build good self-esteem and self-confidence, whether bad stutter days or good ones, they will get through it and be better. - Solange (South Africa)

Depends on my relationship with this person. If it were a friend, I would tell them the truth. There's room for improvement, but you can never be 100% sure. I can be honest with my friends enough to be upfront. If this were a client's mother or father, I would always give them hope that they can improve. I work with autistic children and adults, and I would never tell the parents the whole truth. They need that hope to keep going on days they feel they can't anymore. It's horrible to feel you failed your child. - Samantha W. (Philadelphia)

Do you ever get used to having a stutter?

Yes and no. When you have been stuttering for most of your life, as I have, you know it is a part of you and will continue to play a role in your life. Acceptance can help lessen some of the negative emotions associated with a speech disorder. Still, they never really become "invisible" to the point that you don't notice them, at least in my experience.

Speaking is a very personal act, and how you communicate has a massive impact on how you perceive yourself and by others. Unfortunately, having a stutter still has negative beliefs and perceptions attached to it.

Blocking while making a sound, taking longer than usual to respond, or having an unusual way of communicating can be a surprising experience for the listener. If you have 10 to 20 speaking situations over a day, you will have the same number of "reminders" that your speech is not "normal." That YOU are not normal.

Over the years, I've become much more comfortable with myself, and I even do public speaking for pleasure—something I never expected to say. However, I have never "forgotten" that I stutter. It's there every day, and it still frustrates me when I'm not expecting it or have time pressure to say something.

I'm pretty used to it. That doesn't mean I don't get pissed off now and then, but it doesn't drive my self-esteem into the ground, and I don't hide from it anymore. Bigger things are going on in my life right now. - Shannon C. (Onoway, Canada)

I've knowingly had it for over 70 years. It's who I am. It may have helped me from becoming a bad person. With fluency, I could have been an influencer for no good. - Larry B. (Pittsburgh, PA)

I'm almost 50 and have accepted it as part of my life. I wouldn't say I like it, and it still embarrasses me occasionally, but this, along with my other imperfections and scars, makes me feel FLAWESOME, or so I like to think. - Tesha S. (Croatia)

Yes. Though I stutter on almost every single word in all situations, I hardly think about it. It is not in my mind when I encounter a problem or have to do something. I know I will stutter, and it's not my favorite thing, but I don't feel strong emotions about it or situations in which I have to speak a lot. I have so much other interesting stuff to think about and be busy with, and I know from experience that people love and respect me for who I am. For me, acceptance, being open about it, and not letting my stuttering control my life were key factors. And that I am very passionate about making music and music education and that I could make my hobby my job and vice versa- Mark W. (The Netherlands)

Does stuttering run in your family?

In my case, no. As far as I know, I am the only one, but stuttering has a genetic component, and it's likely to run in families. Thanks to my involvement with the stuttering community worldwide, I've met several people with relatives who stutter. I've also encountered interesting cases like twins where one stutters and the other doesn't. I used to date a girl who stuttered, and she had a brother, a father, and a grandfather who stuttered; the stuttering gene was very strong in that family!

Something else to consider when answering this question is that we are now just barely defining and understanding stuttering. I might have had relatives who stuttered but never addressed it or called it that. Maybe the "uncle that never said a word" was that way because he was covert or scared of opening his mouth.

However, it's also worth mentioning that a family history isn't necessary for stuttering to develop.

Are you aware that you are stuttering when you stutter?

According to my family, I started stuttering when I was under two years old, but I only remember it once I was in school (six to seven years old). Since then, I haven't been able not to be aware of it. Stuttering, particularly blocks, can feel like you are trapped inside your head. You know what you want to say, but the words just don't come out, which can be an incredibly frustrating experience.

Depending on the situation, I might see the word I want to say on my mind's screen and think of how I want to say it, but the sound might not come out; it's like a kind of paralysis. My mouth can make involuntary movements or repetitions. If I can't say the word, I might try to find a different way of saying it that might be effective. I might take a breath and restart. I could gesture to my listener to convey that I'm trying to speak. I might look away because I'm embarrassed by the whole situation. I might look in my brain for synonyms or workarounds to what I'm trying to say (this is called circumlocution). The truth is that every situation is unique, but they rarely are pleasurable or something you are willingly doing. You don't choose to do any of this.

Stuttering can be physically and mentally exhausting because speaking becomes this very complex and elaborate dance where you try to outsmart your brain into not stuttering. Also, you are doing this dance in front of others daily, usually while grappling with shame or embarrassment.

You may also be aware of it before it happens, which only serves to up the anxiety, which in turn makes it more likely that you will stutter.

On top of that, I was only sometimes aware of my secondaries: the gestures, tics, and involuntary movements your body does while you stutter. Over the years, friends (or enemies!) have pointed some of them out, and while embarrassing, that increased my awareness. Sometimes that helps control them.

> *That's the worst part for me. I know it's happening and can even anticipate it, but I often can't stop it. - Allan P. (Manitoba)*
>
> *Always. I find it hard to imagine someone not being aware when they are stuttering. - Christa B. (Dallas, TX)*
>
> *On regular days, I don't focus on it; I talk, but in special situations, yes, of course, I become very aware of it. - Soha E. (Alexandria, Egypt)*
>
> *I stutter more when I'm mentally exhausted and I am entirely aware of it. It really annoys me. - Caesar P. (New Mexico)*
>
> *No. I stuttered until my 20s and most of the time, I was unaware of it. I was only aware of it because others had said something about it. I only remember a few moments when I felt a block coming up. Sometimes, it still happens, and I am only aware of it because my husband (who also stutters severely) likes telling me that I stuttered. - Ellen K. (Netherlands)*

> *I used to kind of blank out. I knew I had stuttered, but there was some deep denial involved. Now, during the actual stuttering, I'm present. There are many things I think and feel according to the day. I know why I'm stuttering more and I can adjust it with whatever needs to happen. This usually deals with projection and slowing down. Giving myself the space to say what I want to say. The important part is catching myself. I've improved with this greatly over the years. - Amey H. (Indiana)*

Do you frequently get unsolicited "advice" from people who don't stutter? Do you find it condescending or patronizing?

ALL THE TIME! Now that I am older, I understand that it comes (mostly) from good intentions and a desire to help, but internally, I still find it a little condescending. When somebody tells me to "just breathe" or "relax" (as I have never thought of that before), it feels like telling a blind person, "Have you tried squinting?"

Something common is people going into story mode and telling me about their relative, neighbor, or classmate who stuttered and cured himself via the X or Y method. I understand it's a way for people to relate to me and show empathy, but it is usually not helpful.

My advice for listeners is always to be patient and kind. Then, if appropriate, ask the person you are talking to how they would like you to react to their stuttering.

> Yes, it's very patronizing. Honestly, it bothers me when I get it from people who stutter. I am a mental health therapist, and usually, people can't stop being anxious on a dime. I don't even know that stuttering is necessarily related to anxiety. Still, to the extent that it is, I find it pretty simplistic to give advice that boils down to "stop being anxious." It's much harder said than done. - Jennifer M. (Tennessee)

> *In my experience, there are a lot of cultural differences between how people in North European countries communicate with people who stutter and how people in the US do. During the 10 years I traveled through almost all of the US, when I played in an international big band, I nearly got advice and comments on my stuttering daily. I got advice from hotel receptionists, airport officials, people laughing at me right in my face, people asking me if I forgot my name, and so on. These things didn't happen to me often in the Netherlands, where I grew up and lived. Sometimes, I encounter people who tell me that I should sing instead of talk, mainly after I give a concert, but I find it irritating, patronizing, and rude. Mark W. (The Netherlands)*
>
> *Yes, and some have a horrified look on their face. Many people slow their speech and use small words like I am stupid. I have had people treat me this way my whole life. It is sad, but I am used to it now. - Lee K. (Orlando)*

Is there something that a communication partner can do to make conversations easier for you?

For me, the key concepts are patience, kindness, and respect. Have patience when the person in front of you stutters. Nothing can make a person who stutters more anxious than a listener who looks distracted, in a rush, or annoyed. Avoid finishing their sentences and maintain eye contact to signal attentive listening.

If uncertain, ask questions with genuine curiosity and respect. However, understand that individual preferences may vary, so avoid generalizing one person's preferences to others.

> *Just be patient and listen well. - Paul G. (Norway)*
>
> *Only finish my sentences or speak on my behalf if I ask you to. Even some of my closest friends do it, and it's infuriating. - Juha (Canada)*
>
> *If I am stuck, I am okay with someone helping me say a word. This is a personal choice. Some PWS do & some don't. I ask my PWS friends if they want help if they're struggling. - Alexis P. (Coventry, UK)*
>
> *Don't finish my sentences. My nephew is bad about this but says it looks painful, so he's trying to help. This makes me think that maybe I shouldn't get mad when a stranger does it, but it's still aggravating. - Matthew M. (Grandin, MO)*

What are some of the techniques you've learned that have helped you the most?

In my particular case, slowing down my speech rate is the most helpful thing to control my stuttering... yet it is incredibly difficult to do it in the middle of a conversation. We live in a world where every second matters, and taking longer to produce sounds can be the difference between being heard and being ignored. As a person who stutters, you quickly become painfully aware of this. Also, speaking slowly and methodically sounds "better" to the listener, but it requires much effort and focus for me. I would describe it as walking somewhere but having to be aware of every step and every muscle needed to make your legs move; yeah, you might never trip, but it makes walking a tedious chore.

Regarding the mental aspect, what helped me the most was to stop thinking of stuttering as this terrible thing that would prevent me from achieving everything I wanted. Once I met other people who were older and more successful than me, I realized that anything and everything was possible. That was a game-changer, and I don't think you can get to this point alone.

I am also a big proponent of sharing that I have a stutter immediately. Growing up, I couldn't imagine myself being comfortable telling everybody that I stutter, but over the years, I have realized that putting my stutter front and center –and naming it stuttering— dispels any misconception about what is happening when I can't produce a sound.

Not talking about your stuttering with the listener causes "the stuttering elephant in the room." If you are like me, the stuttering is evident; it's there no matter if I mention it or not, but not saying anything creates this tension where I try to pretend I am fluent, and the listener pretends not to notice there's something "odd" about what is happening. Being upfront creates a base of understanding, making the conversation a little easier.

Besides that, things like practicing daily meditation, not drinking too much caffeine, or getting good sleep make a difference in my daily fluency. Stephen Pressfield, author of *The War of Art,* has a famous phrase that always resonated with me: *"Of all the people you will know in a lifetime, you are the only one you will never leave or lose. To the question of your life, you are the only answer."* People who stutter must learn to be their own clinicians and experiment with what works specifically for them. How do you feel after drinking coffee or alcohol? Are there any supplements that help your fluency? Does slowing down help you? Are you willing to join a public speaking class? We are all unique, and your specific recipe for success might be different than mine, but you must find out!

> *Knowing that people care less about stuttering than you think they do. What you say is much more important than you stuttering on it. Less worrying promotes your mental health, speech, and confidence. Stick to a speech program and think of it as physiotherapy that you need to keep functioning as well as possible. - Mohamed K. (Egypt)*
>
> *Stop worrying about it. - Stephanie C. (Murrysville, PA)*

I don't know if it's a unique technique, but sometimes speaking slowly helps me not have the blocks or reduces the blocks, but it's challenging to slow down the average speed level of speaking. It works for me sometimes, but not every time. - Towshik A. (Pakistan)

Voluntary stuttering is one of the best things that I still use. It takes the fear out of being stuck on a word. - Mary W. (Burlington, Ontario)

Maintaining eye contact. - Frederick G. (Sacramento, CA)

A big one was to stop rehearsing in my head what to say and learn to speak spontaneously. Being ok talking to myself, hearing my voice and fluency. - Tim G. (Riverview, MI)

Use a DAF (delayed auditory feedback) app to change your tone of voice. - Emad H. (Saudi Arabia)

Acceptance was the gateway to my healing. Desensitization, being willing to show my stuttering, was the next. Over the years, techniques have evolved for me. I view them like another language. I turn them off and on, slipping in and out when I want. My best is just talking and bouncing off the first letter I hit and saying the rest of the word. My natural stuttering is very different from my anxious, fearful stuttering. - Amey H. (Indiana)

I need to take a full breath and read the words in my head while I say them. Takes practice. - Jerome H. (Atlanta, GA)

How does stuttering affect your social life?

As a kid, I was as social as everybody else, at least on the outside. I was invited to parties, and I had a good group of friends, but on the inside, I always felt like I was not part of the conversations. I don't know if they ever noticed or would agree with my assessment of those interactions, but the important thing was that I felt alone, even if I was with others. I remember getting back home and feeling somehow defeated for not saying what I wanted to say.

Growing up, my social life didn't change much. I still had a solid group of friends I would hang out with in school and outside of it, but I still felt like more of an observer than an active participant. I had jokes I never told and stories I wanted to share that I kept to myself. I was pretty much that way until my late twenties.

When I started going to speech therapy, I was forced to address those issues. It was when I began to talk more and engage in more conversations with others in social settings. Nowadays, it's an entirely different story. I am undoubtedly the most social person in my group of friends. Once I got the confidence to start talking and slowly realized most people didn't care, I became the social person I wanted to be since I was a kid. I also began to put effort into developing and nurturing my relationships. It took me many years, but now I can honestly say my stuttering doesn't affect my social life, and if it does, it's not in a negative way.

How has stuttering affected your intimate relationships?

Around middle school, I hated Valentine's Day because I was usually too scared to tell anybody I liked them; it was frustrating. I remember writing letters to girls and never delivering them or just playing imaginary conversations in my head that never became a reality. It was stupid because I remember having a lot of female friends, and some of them would openly tell me things like "so and so thinks you are cute" or other not-so-subtle hints, but I wouldn't do a damn thing about it. I didn't have my first kiss until I was 15, and I spent most of my 20s being single. This is not unusual in the stuttering community.

It wasn't until my late twenties that I finally came out of my shell and realized it wasn't as big of a deal as I thought. If somebody likes you, they usually want you no matter what. I've been in several long-term relationships with women who didn't see my stutter as an issue but have mentioned it as one of their favorite things about me. They have said that it taught them patience and to be a better listener.

The woman I was dating most recently told me early on that she didn't like texting (my favorite method of communication), so when she wanted to talk to me, she would pick up the phone and call me. I think in my early twenties, that would've terrified me. I would've found reasons to always "be busy" and never pick up, but instead, I got so used to it that hearing my phone ring and seeing her name used to make me smile.

Ultimately, I learned that people want and admire authentic people, and stuttering confidently can be super attractive in a world of fake people pretending to be perfect.

It's important to mention that first dates (like work interviews) are also the perfect opportunity to demonstrate that you are comfortable with yourself and put your stuttering out there. Most people appreciate these moments of vulnerability, and they help pave the way to getting to know one another on a deeper level. Now I know that even though stuttering can still make that very first impression a negative one, in the long run, it is only an obstacle if you let it be one.

> *In my early years, I only really talked to women if I had a few drinks. I was timid. But you reach a point where people's expectations and opinions of you, which you cared so much about, no longer matter, and you can be yourself. I have been in two long-term relationships, and in the one I'm in now, we speak about everything. We talk daily, on the phone, in person, for hours. We are getting married next month, and I plan on making a big speech. The moment you realize your words are worth the wait and what any other person thinks about your speech isn't your business, then you are free. - Jeff M. (Australia)*
>
> *It never had an effect. I was fortunate. I had a huge and supportive family, which led me to choose supportive friends and partners. It all led to a belief that my stutter was like a superpower. Seriously. It is the perfect 'asshole detector.' If whatever they gave off made me feel that I couldn't be me, I moved on. - Christopher G. (Philadelphia)*

I struggled in my late teens and early twenties until a woman I had one or two dates with told me on the phone that I had 'a stuttering problem'. That made me realize that pretending the elephant was not in the room was not a good strategy. From then on, I was more upfront about my stuttering, and suddenly, I was more comfortable and more successful (even though I don't like using that term when it comes to dating). If I were to accidentally meet that woman who told me I had a 'stuttering problem,' I would thank her for making me realize that I did not manage my stuttering properly. - Jean-François L. (Montreal, Canada)

I have been married for 42 years to my husband, who stutters nearly every word. His stuttering didn't bother me at all. He was and still is the love of my life. Before me (we were 23 when we met), he already had many girlfriends, and it still seems that he has honey on his butt. So many women find him attractive that I often say I am fortunate, not jealous. I was very impressed by how he dealt with his stuttering. He talked very openly about it and was very confident and communicative. And that matters much more than the severity of his disfluencies. - Ellen K. (Netherlands)

In the past, it affected my intimate relationships very much. I didn't want to be involved in situations with that person's family. There were also so many times I pulled away from friends and lost contact. I was so fearful and ashamed. I didn't know how to live with stuttering; I only knew how to run and hide. I live much differently these days with the help of people who showed me a different way. - Amey H. (Indiana)

I never dated any women before the internet era. I started approaching and 'talking' to women only when online chatting became available. - Ahmad S. (Indonesia)

My stutter knocked my confidence down when I was younger. I was afraid to approach women because I feared stuttering and getting laughed at. The times I gathered courage and talked to women, I was successful, but there were only so many of those times. To give my exes credit, my stutter was never the issue that ended those relationships. Today, I am married to a woman who compliments me perfectly, and we have two beautiful kids. - Josh B. (Milwaukee, WI)

Has stuttering affected your professional life?

Absolutely, in both negative and positive ways. Growing up and into my thirties, I had the idea, which many people who stutter have, that I would never have the job I wanted because of my speech. I thought nobody would hire somebody that struggled to say his name. I would not apply to jobs I wanted because I feared rejection. I lived in what a friend calls "the stuttering closet." Until my thirties, I was severely under-employed, taking low-paying jobs (warehouses, overnight shifts, etc) as long as they didn't require me to talk to people.

Nowadays, the story is very different; I see the many positives stuttering has brought to my life. With time, I grew more confident and realized that as a professional photographer, my work can speak for itself. Also, with hindsight, I can trace my talent as a photographer to the many years I spent quietly in the background of conversations. I became good at reading people and "analyzing the scene," and I became a good storyteller without using words. If you are a good visual artist, you truly can say a thousand words with an image, and I have embraced that.

Aside from that, thanks to my involvement with the *National Stuttering Association*, in 2019, I was approached by another group called *To Be Like Me*.

To *Be Like Me* (www.tobelikeme.org) is a Dallas-based nonprofit that teaches school-age children about disabilities with programs taught by people living with those disabilities. Working with them, I can educate around 50 to 100 children a week about stuttering and how they can help classmates and friends who stutter. This is an opportunity that was only possible because I stutter. This book wouldn't exist, either.

A significant part of who we are is what we believe we can be, and once I stopped believing stuttering was "the worst thing about me," it stopped being just that, and doors started to open for me.

How has having a stutter affected getting hired for a job?

I would argue that 100% of people who stutter have experienced some discrimination or negative experience regarding the job interview process. We live in a world where first impressions can be the difference between getting the job or not, and when you stutter, you are more likely to give away a misleading or harmful first impression.

An interview is putting yourself up for judgment from a person you just met, and stuttering, still to this day, has a negative connotation that can affect your chances of getting the job.

A handshake can be the most distressing scenario imaginable when the person in front of you is expecting you to say your name within a second of shaking hands; a failure to do so can look like you are excessively nervous or unprepared. People asking, *"Did you forget your name?"* are more common than you think[5], and it is very demoralizing when the listener moves on or leaves before you can introduce yourself. Taking longer than "normal" to answer routine questions looks bad, and having a long block can trigger a chain reaction of stuttering instances that can ruin an interview.

Discrimination also can play out differently in different cultures.

---

[5] Seriously, don't do that.

While in some countries it can be illegal to discriminate during the interview/hiring process, there are countries where those kinds of protections don't exist, and discrimination tends to be more prevalent.

All these cultural differences play a part in how we see ourselves, and it's essential to get acquainted and prepared to address your stuttering in an interview.

I try to put my stutter on the table right away. Since I will likely have a block within the first few seconds of the interview, I like to start mentioning what stuttering is, usually with a joke or a touch of humor. People mirror your behavior, and if you look embarrassed or apologetic, it gives the impression that you are uncomfortable about it, consequently making your interviewer uncomfortable. Talking about your stutter with knowledge clears misconceptions, puts you in the driver's seat, and shows you are comfortable and knowledgeable about yourself. This serves the purpose of educating your future employer about what stuttering is and is not. Hopefully, this will clarify that stuttering is just a tiny part of you, but it won't affect your performance at work.

In my case, I also use this opportunity to mention my involvement with stuttering support groups, talk about how I am invited to speak at universities, and so on. This is powerful because it shows I have cultivated unique leadership qualities *because* of my stutter.

I am a massive proponent of openness and honesty, but I must also mention that I didn't always feel this way. When I was younger I still couldn't admit that I stuttered, so having these conversations with strangers was unthinkable– I was not there yet. It took me years of therapy, courage, and practice to be able to talk with a stranger about my stutter confidently.

A fantastic quote about openness comes from Larry Molt in his book *Advice to Those Who Stutter:* "Openness lets in the sunlight that melts the iceberg."

> An HR representative from a reputed firm refused to schedule an interview because I had a stutter. She stated, and I quote: 'Your profile is good, but the manager may not be comfortable taking the interview.' - Shampath S. (Riyadh, Saudi Arabia)
>
> My husband is a professional musician who played for ten years as a trombonist and vocalist. They performed all over the US and Europe, and he never had problems with his stuttering. Later, he applied for a job as a music teacher at a music college in the Netherlands. His interview was horrible; they only asked questions about his stuttering, so after 45 minutes, he said, 'If you can't talk about any of my other qualifications besides my stuttering, I'm stopping this interview.' When he came home, he was sure that he should not get the job, but as surprised as we were, he got hired because they liked that he was so assertive. He worked for 30 years as a teacher and was named 'Teacher of the Year' a few years ago. I think the key to success is accepting yourself as someone who stutters and being assertive and conscious of your qualities. Show people that you are comfortable with your stuttering and that your stuttering is not limiting you, and they will believe that you will be a good match for the job. - Ellen K. (Netherlands)
>
> During an interview a few years ago, I mentioned that I stuttered upfront, and one of the interviewers walked out and didn't return. I didn't hear from them again. - Derek M. (Atlanta, GA)

I graduated from Northwestern University's Kellogg Graduate School of Business with honors. Companies wrote me letters asking me to interview with them; however, when I did interview with them and could barely talk, they all lost interest. I applied for jobs with the Federal Government. I had a GS-11 rating with a score of 95, but after interviewing, no agency would hire me. I still wanted a job and tried for a GS-9 position, but no government agency would hire me again. - Frederick F. (Evanston, Illinois)

The only time it has affected me was when I started to avoid words and not stay true to what I intended to say. I've found that my thinking and ability are transparent to the interviewer if I stutter but don't avoid words. In my experience, people are, for the most part, very understanding and empathetic. - Dan S. (Sidney, Australia)

It's not a coincidence that I've never been hired when I have to do a phone interview. I remember one in particular when I felt so bad because I'm sure the people must have thought I was on some substance. I had blocks and repetitions all over the place. - Briana P. (Dallas, TX)

I had to fight for my Master's degree as the Speech and Hearing Sciences professors told me I couldn't pursue my career in audiology. It sucks, but the only thing to do is keep moving forward. - Peter L. (East Northport, NY)

When you talk with others who stutter, does their stuttering influence yours?

The first time I heard someone stutter in front of me, I was a little uncomfortable because I could feel his blocks in my chest and abdomen. I knew exactly what he was going through; my body was mirroring his tension, and I wanted to help when he was blocking. I also wanted to complete his sentences, which I hate!

My first support meetings with the *National Stuttering Association* made me more aware of the different types of dysfluencies and levels of severity. I discovered "stuttering envy" (I wish my stuttering were like his!) and its opposite, "stuttering pride" (Well, at least I don't talk like THAT!), which were feelings I never had before. Meeting other people who stutter gave me a variety of perspectives that helped me understand myself more.

When I was the leader of my local NSA chapter, our monthly meetings were one of my most dysfluent days. I knew nobody there would judge me, but it still bothered me a little because I wanted to show leadership skills and proficiency, but I ended up sweating and stuttering all over the place. They never seemed to mind, but I still felt embarrassed and tried to be fluent more than usual.

Over time, I have come to accept my stutter, but I still feel slightly uncomfortable listening to somebody else stutter, especially if they are very severe.

I have a friend who stutters, and when I speak with him, I tend to slow down and relax more and rarely stutter. When he speaks, he doesn't try to hide it. I feel for him when he blocks, knowing what he's going through. - Michael H. (UK)

I have found that my stutter magically disappears many times. Could it be that I feel safer in those situations? Probably. - Amey H. (Indiana)

A hundred percent yes. My speech pathologist wife says most people who stutter have strong mirroring neurons. - Doug M. (Wisconsin)

I took a week-long stuttering course here in Ireland a few years ago. It was good to meet some fellow stutters, but I found my stutter got worse when I talked to them. I could hardly string a sentence together. I'm still trying to understand why that was. - James N. (Ireland)

Do you think your life would be drastically different if you didn't stutter?

Absolutely. The voice is very personal, and having trouble communicating "normally" makes you instantly aware that you are different. Feeling different from an early age makes you act differently. When I was growing up, I always thought that I was not the real me. I saw myself as outgoing. I wanted to have many friends. I wanted to feel "part of something," but because of my stuttering, I kept to myself. Even if I knew the answer, I wouldn't raise my hand in class. I wouldn't ask the girl out because I feared rejection. I didn't join the speech class because I knew it would be a disaster, even though I REALLY wanted to do those things. There are many examples, and they are all over my life. I wouldn't be who I am today if I had not grown up with a stutter.

If you had asked me years ago, I would've said my life would be infinitely better without the stuttering. Now, I am not so sure. Maybe I could've taken more chances, but experiencing rejection made me more resilient and compassionate. I may have talked more, but not being able to speak as easily was what made me good at visual arts. It's difficult to say where I (or anyone) would be without stuttering, but it's hard to deny that it has had a massive impact on my life and decisions.

A definite benefit of stuttering was discovering my community. When I started attending meetings of my local chapter of the National Stuttering Association, I felt welcomed into a new world.

For the first time, I saw my stuttering not as something that made me different from everybody else, but instead, it was the one thing that connected every one of us in that room. We all had horror stories about phone calls, drive-thrus, and feeling anxiety when we knew it was going to be our turn to read out loud in class. It was heartwarming not to feel alone anymore.

Those support groups were how I went from "I stutter" to "WE stutter," and I haven't been the same since. This book would not exist without the help of hundreds of members of my stuttering family, my Stamily.

> *Without stuttering, I don't know where or what I would be doing. I've always loved art because it gave me a chance to express what I wanted to say effortlessly, but had I not been given a stutter, I don't know if that would be the case. I always think about this, but I can't picture it. It would be great if I didn't struggle every time I tried to say something, but I can't imagine it any other way. - Cassidy M. (Texas)*
>
> *I probably would have talked more in school and made more friends. However, the funny story is that I accepted a low-level job in my late 20s that didn't require much communication, and that's the workplace where I met my wife. If I didn't stutter, I would never have applied to this company, I would never have met my wife, and my kids would never have been born. - Anthony D. (San Diego)*
>
> *I like the person the hardship has made me. I wouldn't have turned out the same way. I did let my stutter hold me back professionally, but not personally. - Linda S. (Indiana)*

Yes, I would have achieved more, but maybe I would have been dead saying exactly how I feel about things and people. I hate injustice and intimidation, and maybe without a stutter, I would have gotten in trouble. - Chijioke O. (Uturu, Nigeria)

Stuttering has made me more motivated and dedicated. I can tackle many things in life, and where I see people being afraid to take a chance, I'm ok with it because I know things will always work out. – Henryk S. (New York)

My life would be vastly different - not better, but different. That's an important distinction. Stuttering has, for better or worse, influenced many of my life's decisions, and has helped shape the paths and directions of my life - bringing about a lot of interesting twists and turns. If I was a fluent person, my life story would be much more straightforward and much more predictable; and I would even say less interesting! It wouldn't be the unusual life story that I have today. – Paul G. (Norway)

Did stuttering affect your temperament growing up?

Yes. Growing up, I always felt like an outgoing extrovert playing the role of an introvert. My mom is the kind of person who can make friends wherever she goes. She can walk into a room full of strangers, and within minutes, she has everybody laughing because she is telling a funny story. I admired that and wanted to be like her, but I thought that because of my stutter, that was beyond my realm of possibility. It took me until my thirties to be comfortable showing who I am. I am now constantly referred to as the most social person by my friends, and that's a more accurate representation of who I always wanted to be.

In trying to avoid speaking situations, I got into solitary activities like reading, listening to music with headphones, riding a bike, and drawing. I was also into sports like basketball or soccer, where speaking is kept to a minimum, and you show your abilities by playing.

Not letting your stuttering control some of your decisions is very difficult, especially when you are young. On the positive side, stuttering made me a good listener, observer, resilient, and more empathetic person. I can't say it was all bad.

Of course. I avoid people unless it's necessary. I avoid arguing. Stuttering makes me an introvert, while I am an extrovert inside. - Ahmad S. (Malaysia)

No, I was who I was. - Brianna P. (Dallas, TX)

I became a complete antisocial introvert. I also developed a nasty temper, as likely to take a swing at you as say hello. I didn't get a handle on my temper until I was in my 20s. What changed was that I finally found someone patient enough to listen AND honest enough to tell me when I was being a jerk. She became my focal point, something to remember and calm me down whenever I felt like breaking something. Thirty-three years later, she's my wife, and I don't rage out anymore. And yes, I still stutter. - Phil T. (Hendersonville, TN)

Yes, I was always uncomfortable around people and kids my age and didn't trust anyone. It affected my ability to develop meaningful friendships with others. - Anthony D. (San Diego, CA)

If you could give your past self advice about stuttering, what would you say?

I would return to my early teens and tell myself: "Nobody cares as much as you do." I know this is not unique to me or people who stutter, but we all hyper-focus on what we perceive as "flaws" or "differences." We all want to blend in and be perceived as "normal." I always assumed the first thing people thought about me was "the guy who stutters," which was far from the truth. Now I know people see me as artistic, friendly, intelligent, funny, and have many other positive qualities. Stuttering was not even in the top five words most people would use to describe me.

Thanks to my involvement with different stuttering organizations, I've seen that it's absolutely possible to reach this level of acceptance at an early age. Support groups like FRIENDS and the NSA do a fantastic job of teaching young children that it is ok to be different and that people will accept you no matter how you talk. Having a community and knowing you are not alone makes a huge difference. Every time I attend a stuttering event, I am amazed to see children who are comfortable and knowledgeable about their stuttering. Acceptance is a powerful tool!

> *I would return to first grade and tell myself that stuttering is not my fault. I would also tell myself to stop judging myself and talk. I would address the mental gymnastics that I wasted so many years on. - Lisa G. (Brockton, Massachusetts)*

My insecurities stemmed from the ideas others had of my stutter. I'd tell my younger self not to listen to their negativity about my speech. - Young A. (Morpeth, UK)

I would tell myself to stop trying to be a fluent person and be a person who stutters! - Douglas S. (Houston, TX)

I'd go back to my freshman year of high school and tell myself to be bold and try out for that team, jump into new friendships, ask that person out, etc. I adopted this mindset in my sophomore year of college, but I wish I had adopted it five years earlier. - Steve E. (Denver, CO)

I would go back to freshman year, around 14 years old. I would tell myself not to run away from speaking situations. Run towards fear and face it. I missed out on so many things in High School because of fear. But I also didn't know the NSA existed. If I did, things would have been different. - Michele D. (Buffalo, NY)

I would tell my four-year-old self that it's ok to stutter; you're not doing anything wrong, and it's not your fault. Getting that message as a kid would have completely changed my life. No one spoke those words to me until I discovered the NSP (National Stuttering Project, the precursor of the NSA) at age 43. - Lucy W. (Alabama)

Twelve years old, I would tell myself: Claim your voice and tell your story! - Mario S. (Houston, TX)

It's OK to be afraid. Do what you want to do. Push yourself through it. It'll work out later. - Tom S. (Saturn, FLA)

Fourteen years old: Stuttering is FINE. Now listen, the winning lottery numbers are 37... 41... 7... - Casey D. (Toronto, CA)

People want to hear YOU and see the talent that you offer. You don't have to adhere to some fantasy fed to you by culture and the media. - Marc W. (New York)

I'd probably hug myself and say, "Effective communication is not about being fluent. It's about ensuring the other person understands what you're trying to convey. You're great at that. You're a great communicator. Your stutter isn't going to stop you." But I don't know if I'd listen. I was so miserable about my stutter. - Ezra H. (Vista, CA)

Eighteen years old: No one is coming to save you. Stop feeling sorry for yourself; take action because new positive experiences will cancel out your negative ones, and you will begin to believe in yourself again! Put in the work, and you will get results. - Christopher J. (London, UK)

Has your view on stuttering and you as a person who stutters changed over the years? If so, how?

I have shared many examples throughout this book, but the most significant change came when I met others who stutter.

Meeting other people who stutter made me realize that my experiences were not unique and that millions of people felt like me. I immediately stopped feeling alone. Now I am part of an elite club with members from all over the world. Attending events with my stuttering community also allowed me to rub elbows and become friends with many successful people, from doctors, actors, and architects to Oscar-winning writers and everything in between. It hasn't made my stuttering disappear, but now I see it mainly as a positive, which I didn't even consider possible.

> *My view of stuttering has changed repeatedly, but in the end, nothing has changed in how I talk. Only when I accepted that I have a unique dialect (and I deliberately don't say speech disorder) did I start to feel comfortable. No one has to hide or feel bad. The love of our family and friends shows us this. We are ok. - Bernd A. (Germany)*

From my early 20s until my mid-40s, I was obsessed with transforming myself into a fluent speaker, taking fluency shaping program after fluency shaping program, refresher after refresher. I had some successes - I experienced many extended periods of fluent speaking, lasting for weeks or months. The catch was this: I had to intensively practice daily to maintain my fluency. My fluency quickly sank if I slacked off on my boring practice (due to lack of time, motivation, or just getting tired of the whole thing).

Finally, I pulled the plug on the fluency enterprise a little over 20 years ago. I finally accepted myself calmly and peacefully as a person who happens to stutter. And guess what? Life became so much calmer and less pressured. I could now be myself and no longer desired to transform into someone I wasn't. So, I speak differently, that's all. I accept myself as I am. I started to enjoy life. - Paul G. (Norway)

The Dallas chapter of the NSA, 2017

Have you used the Speech Easy or other devices that "stop" stuttering?

Yes. I was 23 years old when my uncle Hector watched a segment on Oprah where they talked about a device called "Speech Easy." Similar to a hearing aid, this device was featured in a segment called "Medical Miracles." I have never watched this segment in particular, but I imagine it showed a person stuttering severely, then a medical professional puts this device in the ear of the patient, and... Voila! Stuttering gone! That's basically how my uncle described it to me and my family.

After watching the segment, my uncle researched and found that the device cost around $5,000, and I had to meet with a speech pathologist to get it. To give some background, my uncle lived in the United States then, but I was still in Mexico, so everything in that story was foreign to me. Oprah? Speech pathologist? Five thousand *dollars*? ¿Qué?

Five thousand dollars was a small fortune for my family, but the idea of a "cure" was incredibly powerful. Within days, my uncle mobilized my family to come up with the money, and I mean my entire family, because he made it his mission to get me this thing and rallied other family members to chip in. A few months later, we had the money and a plan: I would fly to Dallas, where my uncle lived, see this speech pathologist person, get the device... and, I guess, conquer the world or something? I don't think I knew exactly what I would do once I was finally fluent, but I wanted it more than anything.

The day came, and I flew to Dallas to meet this speech pathologist and try the Speech Easy. If you are unfamiliar with the Speech Easy, it is a device you put into your ear and does something called *Delayed Auditory Feedback* (DAF). In simple language, you hear the sounds around you with a delay (that you can adjust on the device). This helps people who stutter in two ways: 1) Listening to yourself speak with a slight delay gives your brain the impression that you are speaking in unison with somebody else. This is called the "choral effect" and generally helps you talk without stuttering, and 2) hearing everything with a delay forces you to speak slower than usual, which, as I have explained before, also helps most people stutter less.

So, what happened when I tried it, you ask? It helped my stuttering a little. That's it.

The reality is that the conditions were not ideal for this device to work for me. First, I was trying it and communicating with a speech pathologist in English, a language I had never used consistently. The cognitive load on my brain was more than usual. Second, it was a very high-stress situation! Many of my relatives had donated money for me to fly to a different country to get this thing, and I didn't want to let everybody down. Finally, I had never had speech therapy before.

The speech pathologist, Mary Irene Burtis (RIP), acknowledged that Speech Easy was not precisely a miracle cure but a tool that could help me increase my fluency. After talking to me for a few minutes, she said that getting the device right away was not something she would recommend.

Instead, she offered me speech therapy to work on understanding my stuttering first, and months down the road, we could try the device again. Unfortunately, I didn't have months because I had to return to Mexico. Still, I appreciated her honesty and attended a handful of speech therapy sessions with her before returning to my country.

This was my first ever experience with a speech therapist, and while it was not the miracle cure my whole family expected, it was helpful. I learned that there were people with actual knowledge about stuttering that could help me. Since I was already in my twenties and just starting therapy, progress was not massive, but I still saw some changes in my fluency and mindset with those sessions.

As far as the Speech Easy was concerned, I could see how it could help because I understood the science behind it, but I also quickly realized that it just wasn't the miracle device it advertised. The device creates the "choral effect" not just with your words but with every sound around you, so I found it very distracting to hear every sound around me twice or with a delay.

It is also known and documented that the brain tends to adapt to these devices, so even if it helps you when you first try it, you have to constantly change the settings (delay and pitch) to keep your brain from reverting to what it feels like normal, aka stuttering.

I find it hard to recommend the Speech Easy to anyone. Not because it doesn't help, DAF works, but you can try DAF using your cellphone and apps on your app store for free or for just a few dollars.

Spending thousands of dollars on something with a track record of being a temporary fix doesn't seem worth it to me.

I tried my first one when it just came out to the public. I was never a fan, and I found it disturbing to hear every sound that delayed. The SmallTalk[6] has a button that you can switch on when speaking and switch off when others are speaking. I used SmallTalk to overcome my fear of the phone, but it didn't stop me from stuttering. Our local chapter bought one for our members to borrow and try it. It's an aid, not a cure, and like everything else, not for everyone. I recommend that people try the free app first and see if it's for you. – Anita B. (Sweden)

The Speech Easy worked for about two weeks before I got used to it. Please don't spend the money; use it for some therapy. Therapy helped more than the device did. - Linda P. (Swanton, OH)

Mine helped me as I practiced 'easy onsets' and prolonging all vowels in words. I no longer needed it two years later, so I passed it on. – Tim G. (Rancho Mirage, CA)

I used a DAF app. It works well with me, especially when I am presenting. It also reduced my anxiety because all you can hear is yourself and your echo. But you have to switch the settings occasionally to keep tricking your brain. - Emad H. (Saudi Arabia)

Yeah, it worked for about two weeks, then stopped. It was a waste of money. – Steve S. (Norway)

---

[6] SmallTalk is device similar to the Speech Easy.

Are there medications that help with stuttering?

At this moment, there is no single medication that can completely cure stuttering. There is some anecdotal evidence that over-the-counter supplements like thiamine (vitamin B1) and magnesium help people who stutter gain increased fluency. However, these have yet to show long-term success for permanent fluency.

Physicians have used certain prescription medications off-label in an attempt to mitigate the symptoms of stuttering, but I recommend doing your homework and only trying something with strict medical supervision. As I mentioned before, I have tried a couple of prescription medications, but none of them were explicitly designed for stuttering, and none of them proved to be particularly helpful to me.

To learn more about the research conducted specifically for stuttering, I recommend reading the book *Without Hesitation: Speaking to the Silence and the Science of Stuttering* by Gerald A. Maguire, MD, and Lisa Gordon Wither (2010).

Dr. Maguire is a professor and chair of the Department of Psychiatry and Neuroscience at UC Riverside School of Medicine. He is a leading researcher in the development of medicinal treatments for stuttering. He is also active in many stuttering support organizations, such as the *National Stuttering Association* and the *World Stuttering Network*.

In his book mentioned above, he shares what has been done to find a medication to help stuttering; however, 14 years have passed since its publication without finding that "magic pill," which tells us there are no easy solutions.

If you could take a magic pill and make your stuttering go away immediately, would you? Why or why not?

This is a fascinating question and something that creates considerable debate in the stuttering community. In my teens and early twenties, I would've taken the pill immediately, no questions asked, because I had the erroneous idea that fluency would fix all of my problems. I used to dream of one day waking up and not stuttering, so of course I would've taken a pill to accomplish that. But then we get into a "butterfly effect" scenario. What are the side effects? Would I be the same person without my stutter? As much as I hated growing up with a stutter, I believe now that stuttering made me empathetic to other people's struggles, a good listener, resilient, and many other good qualities that I don't know if I would've developed otherwise. The magic pill would've robbed me of some formative experiences that made me who I am today.

Today, I might still take the pill, but for different reasons. I am not ashamed of my stutter anymore and can see the multiple benefits that stuttering has brought into my life, but the truth is that stuttering is still exhausting and frustrating. My life would have one less thing to worry about, which makes a difference. I love learning languages, and being able to do it without having stuttering in the back of my mind would be easier, too.

But I wouldn't trade my place in the stuttering community for anything; I have made some of the best friendships ever because I stutter.

I would decline the magic pill. I have found that I have developed positive traits due to stammering, traits I may not have developed without it. I have no regrets. - Malcolm A. (New Amsterdam, Guyana)

I would take it in a heartbeat! I am a stay-at-home mom with three kids. Calling the school, making appointments, attending school meetings, etc., would be much easier without a stutter. No matter how much I accept my stutter, there will always be ignorant people who make jokes and don't understand how genuinely exhausting having a stutter is. I could even talk to my husband without worrying about becoming too mentally exhausted after a simple conversation. - Keyvonna W. (Woodville, Texas)

Of course I would. Stuttering makes my life miserable. Stuttering is not just a speech disorder; it affects everything. We keep all our ideas and comments to ourselves in class because we cannot speak them out. We avoid people, socializing, etc. - Ahmed S. (Malaysia)

No, because I think it would cost me a lot of money! I am a professional singer, and people still see me as the eighth wonder of the world when I stutter on stage and suddenly become fluent when I am singing. It made me famous here, and it is my trademark. But seriously, I would rather my epilepsy could go away. My stuttering doesn't limit me in daily life, not personally and not professionally, but my epilepsy limits me more. The medication also makes my stuttering worse than it already was. - Mark W. (The Netherlands)

It would be one less thing to worry about, but what would the consequences be? Would my personality change, be extroverted, have more friends, get a better job, etc., or would my life be worse than when I stuttered? - Anthony V. (San Diego)

What's the craziest thing you have tried to eliminate your stutter?

When I was twelve, back in México, my mom took me to get a "limpia," the Spanish word for a spiritual cleansing. The "limpia" was performed by a "curandera" (a healer). It took about an hour and involved chanting, burning incense, and praying. At some point, the healer used a couple of eggs, which she rubbed on my neck, mouth, and chest, to " remove the blocks" inside me. I didn't believe it would work, but I went along because I loved that my mom never stopped trying to help me. I did it for her, but maybe I also had a little hope that it would work. It didn't.

When I was in high school, I started to see a new psychologist (probably my third), and he did hypnosis on me to "discover where my trauma began." We had several sessions, and I truly enjoyed the process. I think it helped me work through some experiences I had growing up, like how I handled my parents' divorce and some bullying situations, but I don't feel it had a significant impact on my speech.

Some years later, I visited a psychiatrist, and he recommended trying prescription medications. The only one I remember the name of was Haloperidol, which, according to WebMD, is a medication for Tourette's syndrome and mood disorders like schizophrenia. This was my first time taking prescription medications for stuttering. We tested for two or three months, but it didn't affect my speech much.

Two more things that I thought were crazy but, as years have passed, have become more accepted and mainstream are cannabis and psilocybin. I'll tell you my experiences with both, but before I go any further, I am required to say to you that any depiction or discussion of the use of marijuana, psilocybin, or any other controlled substance should not be construed as advocating, promoting or encouraging the illegal or irresponsible use of such substances. The use of cannabis and psilocybin may be unlawful in your jurisdiction and can have serious legal and health consequences. Furthermore, I accept no responsibility for individuals' actions due to reading this. It is recommended that readers consult with legal and medical professionals for accurate information and guidance regarding the use of any substance. Now, let's get to it.

When I was 25 years old, I started dating this girl who was big into smoking marijuana. Early on in that relationship, she mentioned that once she saw in an episode of a reality show the case of a stuttering person who stopped stuttering after smoking. Until then, I had never tried it and wasn't particularly interested in starting then… but let's say that one night she made me an offer I couldn't refuse (giggity!), and she convinced me to smoke with her. My first experience was filled with a strange mixture of paranoia, giggles, and an insatiable urge to eat everything in her fridge.[7] Sadly, my speech was unaffected.

Nevertheless, one experience a few months later had a lasting impact on me, and I think it's worth sharing.

---

[7] Not a euphemism

One day, we were hanging out at a different friend's house and started smoking a joint. There were six of us in one of those smoking-in-a-circle situations, "That 70s Show" style. After a few puffs, we were all watching TV when I started to get very introspective and think about my life. I noticed that I was surrounded by people, some friends, some strangers, but as much as I struggled to say words, no one in that room ever finished my sentences or made me feel less than them. Everyone accepted me for who I was, and no one saw my stuttering as a reason not to hang out with me. That experience left a lasting impression on me because I think it was the first time I saw my stuttering objectively, without the layers of misconceptions and previous experiences on top of it. Once I was able to put my ego and previous traumas aside, with the help of cannabis, I saw that people didn't care at all how I sounded.

Did it change my life, erase all my bad memories, and turn me into a new man? No. But it did make me question how many of my assumptions were wrong, and I still carry that with me to this day.

Since then, I have smoked cannabis with several people who stutter like me, and some have reported similar experiences. I think cannabis tends to alleviate some of the anxiety you feel before and during talking, and that can help you stutter less, but it shouldn't be considered a cure or a reliable form of therapy. I have not met anybody who stopped stuttering during or after consuming cannabis.

My experience with psilocybin, the active ingredient in "magic mushrooms," is similar to that one. I was 29, and one of my best friends was getting married. He planned a camping trip for his bachelor's party weekend, and I was one of the lucky people invited. Before that day, I had one previous experience with magic mushrooms, but it had been a tiny amount, and it had been a more controlled environment; it was just me and a close friend indoors.

When I got to the camping spot, I realized that I was the youngest of the group by a few years, and I was also a new addition to his group of friends; most of them had been friends for 20 years. This made me feel a little out of place, which made me self-conscious and exacerbated my stuttering (or at least I felt that way). Nevertheless, I talked to everybody, even if I was feeling a little out of my comfort zone.

As the day progressed, we had drinks, grilled some delicious steaks, and made a bonfire. Once it got darker, one of the guys went to his tent and brought back a big bag of mushrooms, which he promptly started passing around. Needless to say, nobody was measuring anything; you got the bag, grabbed a handful of mushrooms, and passed the bag to the next person. I did my part, took a big handful, chewed them, trying not to puke, and around 30 minutes later, I started to feel the effects.

If you are not familiar with psilocybin, the effects vary from person to person and with dosage, but some of the most common ones are feelings of euphoria, sensory distortion, visual and auditory hallucinations, unusual body sensations, ego-dissolution (the idea of self is replaced by a sense of union with all existence), changes in body temperature, and nausea. The effects usually last from two to six hours on average.

My trip included most of those effects: I saw things more vividly, the colors were unusually vibrant, and I felt I could hear the forest come alive. If I closed my eyes, I would see colorful geometric patterns. I felt a sense of bliss.

At some point, we started to gather around the bonfire, and a sense of introspection arose among all of us. We got quiet, and one by one, we retreated into our minds. I was sitting there, contemplating everybody doing their own thing, taking photos, when my brain got caught in what is known as a "thought loop." This is when your brain gets stuck in a chain of thoughts and feelings. What my brain started telling me felt somehow like a pep talk, *"Look around David… nobody cares… just speak… nobody cares… just speak… nobody cares… just speak… nobody cares…"*

I can't tell you how long that went on; it could've been five minutes or an hour, but what I can tell you is that I will never forget that feeling of relief and peace when I heard those words over and over and accepted them as truth.

My friend was getting married, so there was talk of "starting a new phase in life," "turning the page," and so on. The setting was conducive to thinking about making life changes, and thanks to good friends and a little psilocybin, I guess I was in the right frame of mind to do some self-work and rewire my brain a bit. My experience that weekend was also a turning point in my stuttering journey, and my life is better now, thanks to it. I believe I carry the positive effects of that night still to this day.

Nowadays, the study of psychedelic substances like psilocybin is reaching institutions of higher learning like NYU, John Hopkins University, and Harvard, to name a few. While there has not been any research specifically on people who stutter, there have been more than promising results for people with PTSD. A 2013 study from the University of South Florida[8] found that psilocybin stimulates neurogenesis—the growth and repair of brain cells in the hippocampus, the brain's center for emotion and memory. In the study, mice that were given psilocybin overcame fear conditioning far better than mice that were given a placebo. The study supported the hypothesis that psilocybin can help break the traumatic cycle that occurs in patients with PTSD.

I've had several more experiences with psilocybin since then, many of them with the explicit intent of analyzing how it affects my speech. Most of the time, I feel that while I am under the effect of psilocybin, my speech gets considerably worse. I get a general feeling of "shakiness" (my hands tremble, I feel vibrations throughout my body, etc.), which affects how much control I have over my speech; however, I get none of the negative feelings associated with an increase in my stuttering. I also feel more open to having personal conversations about my speech with others. It might be that I usually do these substances in the presence of people I love and care about, but those positive feelings last for months or even years after the experience. This correlates with findings from research in psychedelic-assisted therapy.

---

[8] https://hscweb3.hsc.usf.edu/blog/2013/07/15/low-doses-of-psychedelic-drug-erases-conditioned-fear-in-mice/

If the use of any of these substances scares you, by all means, avoid them. None of these substances were a "magic cure" to my stutter. On the other hand, if you are curious about them, I recommend learning about them from reputable sources and talking to a professional. If you live in a part of the world where this kind of treatment is available and legal, it might be something to consider as a supplementary aid on your journey as a person who stutters.

In my stories and the ones you are about to read, the bottom line is that every person who stutters at some point in their life has told themselves, "I would do ANYTHING to get rid of this." Curiosity and desperation can take you down various roads, some funny, some enlightening, some dangerous. There are also "home remedies" in every country and every culture, but most are not science-based and, on the whole, ineffective. Talk to people, and don't do things you might regret, please.

> *I went to a faith healer when I was eight years old. He sat in a chair, lit a candle, prayed a lot, and had a small broom, which he used to sweep the floor around me. I also had to drink tea, which tasted terrible. It didn't work at all. - Carol C. (Pleasanton, TX)*
>
> *An older relative told me to put a live locust under my tongue. - Jacob D. (San Antonio, TX)*
>
> *Drinking holy water! - Shell S. (United Kingdom)*

When I was twelve and studying for my Bar-Mitzvah, the cantor teaching me told me that another cantor in Europe had told him about a 'cure' for stuttering. The 'cure' was to lie on a sofa for 15 minutes daily, breathe in as deeply as possible, and then hold one's breath for as long as possible before releasing it. At age twelve, I knew nothing about the science of stuttering, and so I religiously followed his advice. My speech didn't improve; my stuttering got worse. After several weeks of gradually worsening stuttering, I finally put two and two together and stopped that ridiculous daily exercise. My speech soon returned to 'normal' for me. - Paul G. (Norway)

When I was a kid, a person from the mountain area of the Himalayas came to our place, observed my stuttering, and suggested eating parrot meat to cure myself. My parents made a parrot once, and I even ate it, but it didn't cure my stutter. - Kamat S. (Delhi, India)

Somebody recommended drinking a large bottle of olive oil with granulated salt and eating holy eggs on my birthday. It was terrible what I suffered at the hands of spiritual healers and pastors in Ghana. - Emmanuel A. (Ghana)

I never tried anything, but I was told to stick a cicada in my mouth, close it, and let it do its thing... supposedly, it works wonders in Mexico. - Ana S. (Ft. Worth, TX)

When I was very young, my mom read about an egg-based cure. We rubbed the egg white on my face and throat and put the yolk under my bed. Supposedly, when I woke up, the yolk would be black. It wasn't. I still stutter. - Stacey M. (Seattle, WA)

> My parents would try anything to 'cure' me. One time, my mom took me to a Muslim priest who said that I was cursed and that he would lift the curse. He gave my mom a piece of paper with words written in Arabic to sew into my undershirt so it was always close to my body. He also said that I had to eat two baked apples every day. To this day, I hate apples and still stutter. - Vesna P. (Croatia)
>
> I used to use Marilyn Monroe's breathy voice when calling the organ bank in the hospital where I worked. It worked. It still does, but I only try it with people who don't know me. - Jacqueline D. (Lincoln, RI)
>
> This is a bit gruesome, but it's part of my story. In fourth grade, I had a plan to cut off my tongue. The plan was made but I didn't go through with it. I feel for that little girl who felt that was her only option. - Amey H. (Georgia)
>
> I heard that somebody got a concussion, and when he woke up, he didn't stutter anymore. I then tried to 'give myself a concussion.' It didn't work, don't do it. - Mark W. (New York)

Years ago, a good friend from the stuttering community named Bernie Weiner, who at the time was in his 70s, got leukemia. After his first chemotherapy treatment, the most surprising thing was that he woke up without the stutter that had accompanied him all his life. Nobody had an explanation as to why this could've happened.

A few weeks later, Bernie and I were chatting, and he, with his great sense of humor, said to me, "*I think I found the cure for stuttering... get cancer!*[9]"

---

[9] Don't get cancer.

Bernie's stutter eventually came back before he ultimately lost his battle with leukemia.

Miss you, Bernie!

Do you stutter in the other languages you speak?

I like to say I am an equal-opportunity stutterer; I stutter in all the languages I speak, but there are a few differences. Speaking is like any other activity; the more you practice something, the easier it gets. My level of fluency usually depends on how often I think/speak in that language. When you have to translate on the fly, you increase the cognitive load on your brain, which means I stutter more in the languages I have less experience with.

I grew up bilingual in Mexico. I started English classes in kindergarten and continued until high school. Eventually, I became proficient in writing and understanding English, but I didn't have many people to practice with; I don't have many memories of speaking outside of the classroom. When I ended up in the United States in my late 20s, it was tough for me to speak English. I had all the words in my mind, but making the sounds with my mouth was a different animal, not just because of my stutter but also because I didn't have much practice. It took me many years to reach a fluency comparable to Spanish.

Nowadays, it's been over a decade since I've been using English as my primary language, and I feel more fluent in English than in Spanish. Most of the media I consume daily and my inner monologue are in English, too, which helps explain my fluency.

Aside from English and Spanish, I have taken German, French, and Danish classes over the years. None of them were particularly easy, but I can say that Danish was probably the hardest, mainly because they make sounds that don't even sound human (I'm joking, Danes!). So far, I have not found a language in which I don't stutter.

> I am a Spanish speaker, but I stutter less in English. I am fluent when learning a new language, but the more I know, the more I stutter. The same happened with French. - Fam C. (Venezuela)
>
> Unfortunately, yes, I stutter in all of them. - Hala G. (Tanta, Egypt)
>
> Yes. When I speak English, I also stutter. My primary language is Dutch. - Petra A. (Netherlands)
>
> I stutter more in English than in Spanish. Spanish is the language I have always used at home. - Jason D. (Gibraltar)
>
> My native language is English. I took some French in high school and college. Stuttered the same amount in both. Probably more with French because I still don't understand it. I can translate it pretty well but can't speak it at all. - Alyssa C. (Normal, IL)
>
> Yes! Living in Wales, I have to say words that start with Ll, which is a sort of choking sound. I live in a village starting with Ll, and I stammer badly on that sound. It's frustrating when I'm trying to catch a bus home! - Mike B. (Wales)

What have been the biggest obstacles to overcome regarding stuttering?

If you had asked me this question a few years ago, I would've had many examples of obstacles, but now that I am older, I think most of them were in my mind and not real obstacles I faced. I would give up or not try things I wanted to try instead of somebody or something stopping me. This brings to mind the following quote by Mark Twain: *"I've suffered a great many catastrophes in my life. Most of them never happened."*

My biggest obstacle was changing my mindset and preconceived ideas about who I thought I was because of my stutter. The people around you tend to reflect what you feel inside, and if you approach people embarrassed or even ashamed of who you are, they will pick up on it. Believing you are capable, worthy, and deserving of good things changes your world. By academic standards, my stuttering is still considered "severe," but my attitude towards it couldn't be more different from how I felt growing up. My life is much better because of that.

That said, it doesn't mean I didn't experience any real-life obstacles. When you are young and facing people in a position of power, it can be difficult. Back in Mexico, when I turned 18, I went to get my first driver's license. During the eye exam, when I was reading the letters from the chart, I had such a hard time saying the letters that the person in charge thought I couldn't see them.

She gave me "the look," and after asking me a few questions I couldn't answer, she denied my application. I was too embarrassed to defend myself, so I walked away feeling defeated. I tried again a few weeks later at a different place, and I stuttered so badly during the process that the person asked me if I had epilepsy or something. Once again, I was denied my license. The person behind the desk said she didn't know if "my condition" would affect my performance on the road. It took me a third time, and my parents showing up to advocate for me, to get my license. I know nobody has a great time at the DMV, but those situations were particularly crushing for my self-esteem.

My first job interviews were also a disaster. I was denied jobs and opportunities countless times. However, **believing you deserve to be heard** is the best and most important step you can take as a person who stutters because it gives you the confidence to defend yourself and prove your worth to others.

> *Developing the courage to make phone calls. When I lived at home, I had my mom call to schedule my doctor appointments, etc. - Michele D. (Buffalo, NY)*
>
> *Maintaining eye contact when I stutter. - Petra A. (Netherlands)*
>
> *Crossing that line from 'Hating my stutter' to 'Embracing my stutter!" - Adam N. (Brentford, ON)*
>
> *Accepting that no matter how you or anyone else feels, it'll never go away. - Ana S. (Ft. Worth, TX)*

It's taken me a long time to realize that I sound better than I think I do. - William T. (Tulsa, OK)

Interpersonal communication skills. I realized I'm stuttering more when addressing specific issues at work, especially when the other person is in charge. I experience a rush of anxiety that affects my speech; I can't comprehend this at all. - Ricardo D. (South Africa)

Obsessing about what other people think about me. - Cilla R. (Jacksonville, FLA)

Learning what the real problem is. It's not stuttering; it's how I feel about myself. I become much more fluent when I feel good about myself. - Jason M. (Louisville, KY)

What are some things you have accomplished despite your stuttering?

I was a good student, even if I avoided speaking situations. I tried harder at everything to compensate for my stuttering, and it usually paid off.

I'm also proud that I took the chance to ask a professor at the University of Texas at Dallas (UTD) if I could attend her classes to learn more about stuttering. She said yes, and now, more than 10 years later, I'm on stage with her almost every week. All those years I spent obsessively thinking about my speech gave me insights I've been able to share with hundreds of future SLPs.

Those years of talking in front of universities made me well-known within the stuttering community. As a result, an organization called To Be Like Me (www.tobelikeme.org) recruited me to be one of the "stuttering experts" for their program. With them, I talk to children weekly about stuttering and how to be more empathetic to people with differences. Stuttering made me a public speaker, and I still find that incredible. It goes to show you how everything comes down to perspective. That thing you hate about yourself might be a strength. That thing you are embarrassed by now might be the thing that makes you recognizable and appreciated later in life.

On that note, my time with Toastmasters has been a significant source of pride. Joining a public speaking group for pleasure would've sounded insane to me as a child, but over more than a decade with the organization, I have given around 60 speeches and won trophies at club and regional levels.

> **FIRST SPAKER** Dena
> Thank you for sharing your experience. Such an inspiration! I admire your courage + I struggle

> **THIRD SPEAKER**
> Very Inspirational. Loved your smile & self confidence.

> **THIRD SPEAKER** David
> OMG! My jaw dropped! You're the man David! The greatest applause I've heard in here. You're a natural leader.

> **THIRD SPEAKER** David
> I can't believe the improvement from the ice breaker! So well delivered & you are an inspiration - Keep enlightening the world!

> **THIRD SPEAKER**
> Amazing!! I will always remember your speech. You are very courageous!

> **THIRD SPEAKER**
> AWESOME JOB! PROUD OF YOU

Feedback I received after my second speech at Toastmasters

Finally, a couple of years ago, I was invited to speak at a middle school in Dallas. That school had five or six children who stuttered, and the speech pathologists who worked there asked me to talk to them about life as an adult who stutters.

Those children had the same fears I had growing up: fear of people judging them, of not fitting in, of not being able to reach their potential because of the way they talk, etc. I hoped to instill in them the idea that most fears exist only in their mind and that most people reflect on what they project. If you feel confident, capable, and powerful, people will match that and treat you accordingly. I also told them the importance of humor and that nobody can use it to hurt you if you can laugh at your stuttering.

One of the speech pathologists' "goals" for the children was to make a booklet about stuttering to give away at their school. The booklet's purpose was to inform the rest of the students about what stuttering is, share with them what it means to live with stuttering, and detail what it means to be "good allies."

A few weeks later, one of the speech pathologists reached out to me and sent me the following photo, saying that the kids had decided to dedicate their stuttering booklet to me.

I would be happy if that's all I ever accomplish in the stuttering community!

From the book "Diary of a fish with a stutter."

Despite my stuttering, I became a nurse and retired after 25 years as a nurse and eight years as a CNA. My stuttering does not define me in any way. It once did, but only for a short time. - Cilla R. (Jacksonville, FLA)

I work for the court system in Boston and am a music producer. I reach out to prospective artists and discuss what I do, find out what they need, and collaborate. I do this on the phone or over Zoom. I don't let stuttering stop me from what I need or want to do. - Mark B. (Stoughton, MA)

I became a university lecturer. Public speaking and changing my perception of my stutter has been life-changing. I no longer let my stutter control me. - Mick B. (Australia)

I'm an audiologist. I talk to my hard-of-hearing patients all day. I've given lectures, taught classes, and am very comfortable speaking to a large group of people. - Peter L. (East Northport, NY)

I graduated from high school, a community college, and a university. I became a Registered Dietitian, and I talk to my co-workers and residents every day. - Michele D. (Buffalo, NY)

I've been a nurse for almost ten years now! I talk to people all day; some days are tough, but I've stopped letting it define me. I've also met other nurses who stutter, some more severely than others, but they are also excellent! We can do anything! - Katie R. (Cincinnati, OH)

I was told I wouldn't be accepted into actor training courses because of my stutter, and then I became semi-successful as an actor. - David T. (Lancaster, UK)

I did what professors told me I couldn't. I graduated with a degree in psychology and went on to a graduate Urban Education program where I planned on teaching psychology. I studied/taught under a man who could not get over my speech. He constantly commented and pointed it out even though the class's grades increased dramatically when I took over and started teaching. The kids got over it. I did what I wanted regardless of the tremendous stress I was put under.
- Amey H. (Indiana)

I was a carpenter, relying on my work rather than my words, but there's no money in that. Now, I am a construction supervisor, and my job requires talking every day, mainly in Portuguese as a second language. My stutter is pretty much a non-issue at this point. – Trevor A. (Boston, MA)

I'm a social worker. Some days are harder than others, but I actually talk to people for a living. – Linda S. (Denton, TX)

Do you stutter in your dreams?

I can't remember a single case of me stuttering in my dreams, but I don't usually remember speaking that much. There was a time, some years ago, when I tried to learn lucid dreaming, and my objective was to practice speaking techniques when I slept, but I never had enough control over my dreams to remember my speech techniques.

> I do, and I usually have negative feelings about it. The last I remember, I disclosed it in my dreams LOL. But I also sleep talk, and speak very fluently - Rudr S. (India)
>
> I don't stutter, but I whisper so I won't stutter. Sometimes, I wake up whispering. Sometimes I need to speak in my dreams and can't. - Amey H. (Indiana)
>
> All the time, even sometimes more than I do when I'm awake. That may be due to shame and fear of judgment from people. - Lindsay N. (Bakersfield, CA)
>
> Yeah, I do. I even stutter when I am talking to myself. Stuttering is in my genes and follows me everywhere I am. - Emmanuel A. (Ghana)
>
> I have stuttered in my dreams before, but it's not often. When it does happen, my stuttering is also more severe in my dreams than in real life. - Brianna P. (Dallas, TX)

If you worked with a speech therapist, what did they do well? What do you wish they had done better?

I only had access to speech therapy once I was in my late twenties, but once I did, the experience was life-changing. I had a brilliant, beautiful human as a speech pathologist, and she transformed me into who I am today. I owe Dr. Freeman a lot.

One of the most meaningful things Dr. Freeman did for me was answer all my questions about stuttering. Having grown up in another country, I had a lot of misinformation and wrong ideas about stuttering and myself. She demystified it for me and made it "something I did" instead of "something that happened to me and I had no control over." That was massive.

Dr. Freeman also made me realize that communication is way more than what comes out of my mouth and that I could be eloquent, persuasive, and entertaining with or without a stutter. Thanks to her, I learned and internalized that communicating effectively involves body language, confidence, content, humor, gestures, etc. While I might not be the best at speaking, I can be a good communicator by focusing on my natural strengths or developing new ones.

I also learned that stuttering confidently in front of a crowd shows vulnerability, and that creates an instant bond with people. Owning our stuttering can be empowering and inspiring for others.

More importantly, Dr. Freeman made me realize the value of sharing my story. Speaking about my experiences in the context of a support group could inspire others to try new things or get out of bad habits. I might be further along in "the stuttering journey" than others, and by being open about my struggles and successes, I could provide encouragement, strength, and hope to somebody looking to improve their life.

This book wouldn't exist without the encouragement of not only Dr. Freeman but many other speech pathologists along the way.

That being said, I have heard some horror stories about therapy, and it's worth knowing what can go wrong to avoid mistakes, both as a therapist and a client. Know that only some speech pathologists get proper training to treat stuttering. Some speech pathology programs do not require their students to take more than one class on stuttering to graduate and practice. So, do a little research before committing to a therapist. Ask questions, ensure it feels right, and seek advice within the stuttering community if you need help. We are there for you!

> *I tried Speech Therapy - Fluency training, stuttering modification therapy, DAF, Drug therapy, and hybrid fluency training/stuttering modification therapy - these types of treatment led me to choose SILENCE rather than feel just as stupid trying to use "therapized" speech as I did stuttering. Know what you want as an outcome for yourself if you go the therapy route. - Michael R. (Wisconsin)*

Therapy helped me identify when I stutter the most and where the tension is. It taught me techniques like easy onset, prolongation, etc., but practicing them in real life was hard. - Dominique D. (Kennesaw, GA)

Different speech pathologists have different approaches. First, ensure the clinician has experience treating fluency disorders (since not all do). The best of them understand the disorder from both the physiological and psychological perspectives and can help by either 1) Teaching you special techniques, such as relaxed breathing and gentle onsets, or 2) Helping you to reduce stuttering anxieties, increase confidence, increase self-acceptance, reduce avoidance, and cope in life as a person who stutters; or 3) A combination of these. - Paul G. (Norway)

I had speech therapy more than 60 years ago when speech therapy was nowhere as effective as it is now. I recommend therapy nowadays. Make sure that 1) It includes a thorough evaluation that results in a treatment plan that is tailored to your needs and 2) The therapist is certified or licensed to increase the probability that you will get someone who is committed to your success. That which works for one person may not necessarily work for the next. Nevertheless, effective treatment will entail numerous hours of hard work and practice. - Robert W. (Bakersfield, CA)

Did you ever have a "breakthrough" moment in therapy?

There were a few, but one of them stands out. Years ago, I tried an intensive therapy program that promised fluency at the end of it. The program consisted of four eight-hour days of therapy with a group of speech pathologists. It was as intense as anything I ever tried, but by the end of the four days, I honestly was 100% fluent. I talked so drastically differently that when I called my mom at the end of the fourth day, in front of all the SLPs, she didn't recognize who I was until a few minutes into that conversation! I felt like a million dollars and imagined everything in my life would never be the same.

The next day, I went to have lunch with a good friend and his wife. In the back of my mind, I expected them to have their minds blown away by my fluency. The reality is that they didn't even notice until 20-30 minutes into the conversation when my friend's wife said, "Hey, you haven't stuttered in a while." I excitedly told them about my intensive therapy program. Their reaction to my big news was akin to "Oh, that's neat!" and we moved on.

That moment has always stuck in my mind because it made me realize that the people around me were not as obsessed with my speech as I was. They accepted me with my stuttering, and after months of knowing me, it didn't even register in their minds anymore. They were more focused on my message than how it came out of my mouth.

In the following days, I also realized that the world around me didn't drastically change. Some people noticed it at work, and some didn't, but I still had the same obligations. It still wasn't my dream job.

More importantly, I realized that even with my newfound fluency, I still had that anxiety when somebody surprised me with an unexpected question or when my phone rang. I had completely changed the way I was talking, but inside, I was still the same person with the same fears. In other words, we didn't even touch the bottom of the iceberg.

My stuttering eventually came back gradually, mainly because I stopped doing the necessary maintenance exercises to remain fluent, but that whole experience made a significant impression on me. I learned from that experience that stuttering was not the first thing people noticed about me or the one thing holding me back. I realized my dreams would not come true because I was fluent.

> *After years and years of therapy, I realized it didn't make a difference at all; it made me more aware of my speech and made it worse. When I stopped worrying about it 24/7... it got better. I still stutter and block hard, but it comes in waves. Sometimes, I can have a whole conversation and not stutter once. Same person, same conversation a month later, I can't get a word out. Outside stressors directly affect how much and hard I stutter, but I don't care nearly as much anymore. It is what it is. - Stephanie C. (Murrysville, PA)*

Two critical breakthroughs marked my stuttering journey. They may seem to be opposites in some ways, but in other ways, the first one helped me indirectly into the second one. The first occurred when I was 33 and attended the Hollins Communications Research Institute to learn the Precision Fluency Shaping Program. After three months of intensive daily practice of these techniques, I achieved what I considered a milestone victory: for the first time in my life, I was fluent in all situations!

This consistent fluency lasted a few months but eventually collapsed. For years, I took refresher after refresher and always managed to bring fluency back into my life, but it inevitably collapsed after a few months back home. I learned that maintaining my fluency required intensive work in daily formal practice and careful monitoring of techniques in all conversations.

And then came the second big breakthrough, which occurred in my late forties. Once I learned that fluency was possible, I had to ask myself if fluency was essential to a happy life… and it wasn't. There is much more to life than to be obsessed with fluency. Life became so much happier for me and so much less stressful when I finally achieved this acceptance. - Paul G. (Norway)

I remember being taken aback that other people didn't always register my stuttering. I'd thought that something so important for me must also be the focus for others, but that was not the case. Also realizing that fluency is nice to have, but you don't suddenly become the favourite for promotions at work, irresistible to the dating pool, or an amazing public speaker. – Max G. (Manchester)

I had two: The first was after attending several conferences of the National Stuttering Association, finally realizing I was never going to be a fluent person and that it was okay. That breakthrough dealt with everything below the iceberg. The second breakthrough was taking a three-week intensive therapy called Precision Fluency Shaping Program, taught by Ross Barrett, a person who stuttered himself. After a week in therapy, I learned so much about what I was doing that got in the way of producing fluent words. The ability to have tangible things I could focus on and do instead of the fear and anxiety of stuttering helped. Over time, I produced more fluent speech by releasing the shame of stuttering and being okay with sounding different when using the techniques. For me, the combination of NSA + PFSP has allowed me to take control of my stuttering instead of letting my stuttering control me. I am not a fluent person, but that is OK. I am a person who stutters. - Doug S. (Houston, TX)

What advice would you give future speech pathologists?

Always be aware that you are working with a human, a unique individual. While you can learn theories and techniques from books, your clients will all be different and come to you from a unique place. Knowing their specific needs and expectations will help you serve them better. Some people will love focusing on techniques, while others might be content just being listened to. Be patient and understand that "rewiring" somebody's brain is a long process. Also, success looks different to different people. While "100% fluency" might be the goal of everyone who walks into your office, sometimes acceptance can have more of an impact than fluency will ever have. Talking about it can make you understand your client's specific needs and the best ways to get there.

I also advocate for a little "tough love" too. When I first started therapy, I thought I knew exactly what I needed and how to get there. I wanted a quick solution to a decades-old problem, and life doesn't work that way. My therapist was very dedicated to helping me, and sometimes that meant she had to be a little tough on me and not let me get away with lazy effort during our sessions.

Speech therapy is complex and tedious, especially when you have been stuttering for many years; successful therapy might include days where you are lending an empathetic ear and days where you are more of a drill sergeant. Don't be afraid to push a little when needed, but make sure you explain the reasoning behind everything. Having a "why" can be a powerful way to motivate someone when they feel like giving up.

> *Refrain from questioning your clients' lived experiences with stuttering. Start at the point where your client is. Please don't assume that everyone who stutters has the same stutter patterns and the same psychosocial problems without asking them. Do an extensive initial assessment before developing a tailor-made therapy program, including emotional and social elements. Be transparent about the therapy approach and the client's requirements. Set realistic goals together with your client. Use a holistic approach, including the cognitive, emotional, and social elements of stuttering. Let your client be the lead in decisions regarding the therapy approach. Take the role of a counselor and not the role of an expert. Know the boundaries of your skills. If you cannot address the psychosocial elements of stuttering, don't experiment, but be open about it and refer to a colleague if needed. Make the transfer to daily life situations an essential part of the therapy program. Offer guidance to prepare for important events, like job interviews and presentations, and how to cope with stuttering in the workplace. Refer your client to support groups. Involve your client's environment in the therapy if necessary. Educate yourself as much as possible about stuttering, and work on your continuing education. - Ellen K. (Netherlands)*

Listen. Understand our anxiety and be flexible on the techniques since they all will not fit our needs. - Gary A. (Chicago)

Join Facebook groups to learn more about how our dysfluency affects us directly from us. - Arthur Y. (England)

Listen. People who stutter are the experts on their stuttering— not us. I teach graduate students and give several tidbits, but that's one of them. – Steff L. (Colorado)

What support does the National Stuttering Association provide to individuals who stutter?

From their website:

> The National Stuttering Association is the largest non-profit organization in the world dedicated to bringing hope and empowerment to children and adults who stutter, their families, and professionals through support, education, advocacy, and research. Our vision is to build upon our position as the preeminent organization for supporting people who stutter.
>
> Since 1977, the NSA has been enhancing the lives of people who stutter, educating the public, assisting speech professionals, championing research, and advocating for reducing the stigma of stuttering.

The NSA is an organization that coordinates several "chapters" in the country (174 at the time of writing this book) aimed to provide support to people who stutter. Most of those support groups serve adults, but there are also groups for kids, teens, and families. The meetings are different depending on the chapter, but generally, they are led by a "chapter leader" who picks a specific topic to discuss during the meeting. Everybody is welcome to chime in with their opinion or perspective.

The topics like "stuttering in the workplace," "stuttering and relationships," and so on can be varied. They are primarily used as conversation starters, but the conversation is free-flowing, and we might talk about something completely unrelated.

The most important thing the NSA provides for kids and adults is a sense of belonging. Stuttering is a rare disorder, and most of us go from childhood through adulthood without ever meeting somebody else who stutters. Being in a room with others who share your experiences can be cathartic.

I never belonged to a support group before discovering the NSA, but my life has been better since I started going to meetings years ago. Aside from the monthly meetings, the NSA has an annual conference where all the chapters across the country and affiliates from around the world get together. It's a week-long celebration of stuttering with workshops, keynote speakers, group activities, and more. I attended my first conference in 2011, and that year, the keynote speaker was David Seidler, the screenwriter for *The King's Speech*. Hearing him tell his story (and how similar it was to mine, no matter the difference in age and background) was pretty incredible. I still quote parts of his speech to this day.

These conferences attract anywhere from 500 to 900 people from all over the world. While it can be a little overwhelming, being in an environment where stuttering IS the norm is a surreal experience that I can't recommend enough. I have tried to attend every year since, and it's very difficult for me to imagine missing one of them.

Aside from the NSA, other organizations provide similar support groups that I would love to mention:

FRIENDS: The National Association for Young People Who Stutter (www.friendswhostutter.org).

SAY: The Stuttering Association for the Young (www.say.org).

The Arthur M. Blank Center for Stuttering Education & Research (www.blankcenterforstuttering.org).

Aside from those organizations, online support groups like Stutter Social exist. Stutter Social (www.stuttersocial.com) provides free online meetings for people who stutter via Google Meet. There are four weekly meetings, and I am proud to serve as one of their hosts. The meetings follow a similar format to an NSA chapter meeting, where a host facilitates conversation among the participants.

If you are a person who stutters, I highly recommend joining one or more of these organizations. Life gets significantly more manageable once you realize you are not alone, and some of the people you will meet in those groups will become friends for life.

Outside of the USA, there are also many organizations like the Canadian Stuttering Association (www.stutter.ca), ABC Begaiement (www.abcbegaiement.com), STAMMA, The British Stammering Association (www.stamma.org), and many, many more.

What continuing education opportunities exist for professionals working with individuals who stutter?

I can't speak much about the specific licensing and continuing education opportunities available to speech pathologists because those vary depending on your location. One thing I can't recommend enough is attending meetings of the National Stuttering Association, FRIENDS, or similar organizations to hear stories directly from people who live with a stutter. Stuttering has some commonalities but can also radically differ depending on age, culture, or other variables. Attending meetings and hearing our stories gives you a variety of perspectives that you can apply to your client's specific needs.

If there is no local chapter of the NSA or a similar organization, I would recommend attending the virtual meetings of Stutter Social (www.stuttersocial.com) or joining groups like "Stuttering Community" and "World Stuttering Network" on Facebook.

To find specific certifications available for you as an SLP, visit the website of the American Speech-Language-Hearing Association (www.asha.org), the American Board of Fluency and Fluency Disorders (www.stutteringspecialists.org), or search for similar organizations in your country.

What resources (books, blogs, websites, etc) have you found helpful?

I don't consume too much stuttering-related media these days, but in my early days in therapy, when I was "starving for knowledge," I found the books from the Stuttering Foundation (www.stutteringhelp.org) very helpful. *A Stutterer's Story, Self-therapy For The Stutterer,* and *Advice for Those Who Stutter* were incredibly helpful in those early days.

Nowadays, we live in a golden era of stuttering resources and have dozens of options for every taste. Some of the ones I can recommend are:

National Stuttering Association. The biggest network of support groups for people who stutter in the US. The monthly meetings of the Dallas chapter changed my life, and the annual conference is still, to this day, my favorite weekend of the year every year. Their website has numerous educational resources, most of them for free. Get connected! (www.westutter.org)

Friends: The National Association of Young People Who Stutter. I am new to this organization, but my first impression was overwhelmingly positive. They do a fantastic job with what I would call a "full family approach." If you are a parent of a kid who stutters, I can't recommend them enough. Their annual conference is one of the most beautiful, heart-warming events I have ever attended. (www.friendswhostutter.org)

Stutter Social. An online support group via Google Meet for people who stutter. Meetings are held 4 days a week, with different hosts depending on the day (I host on Wednesdays). Anybody is welcome to join, and the topics of conversation vary. I have talked a lot about the power of the community, and if you don't have access to a good in-person support group in your community, this is the second-best option. (www.stuttersocial.com)

Stutter Talk. The longest-running podcast about stuttering, hosted by Peter Reitzes and Chaya Goldstein-Schuff. Guests are people who stutter, telling their stories, and specialists share the latest research and therapy approaches. Listening to this podcast can feel like getting a master's degree in stuttering. If you want to learn from the best, this is it. They have more than 700 episodes at the moment of writing this book. (www.stuttertalk.com)

When I Stutter. Award-winning documentary by John Gomez, a professor of Fluency Disorders at Cal State LA and practicing SLP. Having personally met John, I can say that he "gets it" and is one of our best allies in the stuttering community. (https://keeneyeproductions.com/when-i-stutter-documentary)

The Way We Talk. A documentary film by Michael Turner. Michael is a person who stutters and was awarded the 2015 Oregon Media Arts Fellowship for The Way We Talk. The movie shares his journey as a person who stutters and explores speech therapy in places like Japan. (www.thewaywetalk.org)

Stutterology. Blog and podcast created by Ezra Horak, from Portland, OR. Informative and personal, with stories, research links, and more. Ezra was recently one of the keynote speakers at the 2024 NSA Conference in St. Louis, MO. (www.stutterology.com)

JustStutter. A webcomic about stuttering, created by Willemijn Bolks, an artist from the Netherlands. Her comics showcase everyday situations and uplifting messages related to stuttering. I'm a big fan of her style and sense of humor! (www.instagram.com/juststutter)

Proud Stutter. An award-winning podcast about stuttering hosted by Maya Chupkov. Features interviews with people who stutter and specialists. (https://www.proudstutter.com)

Historias de Tartamudez. A podcast about stuttering, in Spanish, hosted by Cynthia Dacillo y Jhoan Gallego. They have one guest per episode who shares about life with stuttering.

Women Who Stutter: Our stories. A podcast about stuttering focused on women and their stories, hosted by Pamela Mertz. (www.stutterrockstar.com)

Dear World, I Stutter. Book by James Hayden. To process his story and accept his stutter, James decided to write a series of open letters to those who have been or will be on a journey with stuttering. These letters provide an honest and vulnerable look into the heart and mind of a person who stutters.

Life on Delay: Making Peace with a Stutter. Book by John Hendrickson. After his award-winning Atlantic feature "What Joe Biden Can't Bring Himself to Say," John wrote this book about making peace with your past and your speech.

My Beautiful Stutter. A documentary film directed by Ryan Gielen and written by Steve Sander. It follows a group of five kids who stutter, ages 9 to 18, attending Camp SAY in New York. Winner of multiple awards, including the 2020 Shorty Award for Social Good. (www.mybeautifulstutter.com)

Out With It: How Stuttering Helped Me Find My Voice. A vividly powerful memoir of a young woman who fought for years to change who she was until she finally found her voice and learned to embrace her imperfection. (www.katherinepreston.com)

Stuttering is Cool. Comic book and podcast of the same name by Daniele Rossi, a Canadian artist and advocate. The book is also available in French. He also has stuttering merch. (www.stutteringiscool.com)

All The Right Words: My Journey as a Sportswriter who Stutters. Book by Ryan Cowley. Ryan is an ambassador for the stuttering community, having spoken about his life and career as a PWS for multiple stuttering-related organizations and Communication Sciences & Disorders and Speech-Language Pathology programs at colleges and universities across the United States and Canada. (www.ryanacowley.com)

Final thoughts

When I first accepted the opportunity to attend my first panel at the University of Texas at Dallas, I had no idea where that would take me. What started as a therapy exercise for me made me reevaluate my life and my relationship with this thing called stuttering. In a few years, I went from wanting to get rid of it at all costs to understanding it, appreciating it, and, in a turn of events I couldn't have imagined, wearing it with pride. Over the last decade I have gone from being very ignorant about this thing I had all my life to considering myself knowledgeable enough to write a book about it (with the help of my Stamily)!

Stuttering made my childhood harder than it had to be, and my adulthood has had some roadblocks because of my inability to communicate "normally," but I can say that stuttering has enriched my life with opportunities and friendships I would not have encountered otherwise.

My main goal with this book is to give you, my reader, as much information as we have about this enigmatic disorder. I firmly believe that knowledge is power, and knowledge can be liberating. The moment I started to get educated about what stuttering is, it began to lose its hold on me. I didn't fear it anymore; I understood it. That change in perspective made a big difference.

That knowledge didn't make my stuttering disappear. I still stutter pretty "bad," but it no longer controls my life. I live a happy life as a person who stutters, and I want you to know that is a possibility— You can do it too!

While this book has many answers, just as many questions remain. As we get better at learning about the brain and its inner workings, we might finally get the answers to the really big questions about stuttering, like its causes and possible cures. In the meantime, I hope this book helps you find your way in life as a person who stutters, as a parent, or as a student looking to become a professional working with people who stutter. This has been a labor of love, and I can genuinely say there's no way I could've done it without the help from many SLPs who "get it" and the support of the stuttering community behind me.

If you stutter, **I hope you realize you can achieve and become anything you want**. Stuttering may make some things harder, but not impossible. Doing hard things is good for you anyway, so embrace those challenges! A change in attitude makes all the difference in the world, trust me. I have seen it repeatedly in myself and others while attending support groups.

You are not alone, and you never have to be. Millions of people are going through the same thing as you, and together we are stronger than ever. I hope that this book gives you the courage to use your voice because the world deserves to hear what you have inside you.

Welcome to my Stamily!

Acknowledgments

This book wouldn't exist without the help of many, many people. It honestly took a village. I can't start this section without acknowledging my mom, who, since day one, supported me and made me feel like I was capable of anything, stuttering or not. She doesn't speak much English, so she might never know what I'm saying here, but trust me, she is the real MVP here. If there is any quality you like about me, it probably came from her. ¡Mamá, Juan Chinguetas escribió un libro!

To Fede, my stepdad, and my brothers Eduardo and Oscar, los quiero caras de burro. Thanks to my uncle Hector, who took it as a mission to help me and inadvertently changed my life by flying me to Dallas for the first time. To my aunts *la China, el Burro, la Güera y Marta* (you need a nickname) for chipping in for that first trip; I have never felt more loved than when I saw how much every one of you cared about me. Thanks to the rest of my family for never making me feel inferior. ¡Los extraño!

Infinite thanks to the holy trinity of speech pathologists who helped and encouraged me the most when I needed them: Mary Irene Burtis (RIP), Frances Freeman, and Jan Lougeay. You transformed me from someone who thought I wouldn't accomplish anything meaningful to somebody who dared to write a whole-ass book in his second language. Thank you for your kindness, patience, and encouragement during the years I've known you. To think I'm just one of hundreds of people you have helped during your illustrious careers is mindboggling. The world is better thanks to you all.

To the National Stuttering Association. You are not the only support group for people who stutter, but you were my first love, and I owe you more than I can repay you. The friends I have met through this organization are some of the world's most beautiful, selfless, powerful people. Special thanks to the mighty Dallas chapter, which is home to some of the most fantastic characters in the stuttering community: Lee, Russ (you'll be remembered forever, my dude), Sivan, Andrew, Jeff, Joseph, Kelly, Ashley, Sufian and many, many more.

To Angela Medina, John Gomez, and Karin Morrison Manchack, some of my favorite SLPs. Neither stutter, but they are the definition and perfect example of an ally. Your help proofreading this book, making corrections, and encouraging helped me keep pushing when I was tired of writing and rewriting.

To my friends, some of whom still to this day give me brutal nicknames because of my speech. You have helped me grow a thick skin and taught me not to take myself too seriously, one roast at a time. Thank you, jerks.

To the stuttering community for helping me during my research and for the years of inspiration. I am proud to be one of you, and I am constantly in awe of all y'alls hearts, courage and resilience. We are the world's best, most elite club, and I wouldn't change it for anything.

I would also thank my buddy Derek Mitchell, but he never took the time to read what I sent him. He's still cool.

About the Author

David Alberto Alpuche Ramírez is a photographer, entrepreneur, and author from Mexico City. He began stuttering at the age of two, and he's pretty good at it by now. David has been active in the stuttering community for more than a decade as a member of the National Stuttering Association (where he was awarded Chapter Leader of the Year in 2017), a consultant at the University of Texas at Dallas, hosting the online support group Stutter Social, and as one of the leaders in the nonprofit To Be Like Me. As a member of Toastmasters, David's speeches have earned multiple awards at Club, Area, and District levels. When he's not working, he enjoys playing chess, reading, and diving into the occasional mosh pit at metal festivals.

1000 Answers: What Everyone Should Know About Stuttering is David's first book in English, but he was also the Spanish translator for Steven Pressfield's cult classic *The War of Art*, available from Black Irish Books.

His website is www.davidthephotoguy.com

Extras

The following is an essay I wrote after winning my first speech contest at Toastmasters, in 2017:

LAST THURSDAY I WON A SPEECH CONTEST AT TOASTMASTERS!!!!!

Can you believe it?! The guy with the stutter winning a speech contest?! While being modest has never been my forte, sharing this story is about more than myself, it's for the many, many people that stutter that I know.

I started stuttering when I was 2 years old and I quickly realized my life was not going to be easy. Introducing yourself, participating in class, using the telephone, talking to friends, ordering at restaurants, asking for that cute girl's number.... EVERY... SINGLE...THING becomes a challenge when you can't trust your voice will be there for you. Stuttering makes talking, that thing you see everybody doing so effortlessly, feels like an enemy, and it can wreck your mind and confidence. I hated talking. With a passion. So how do you from that to winning a speech contest? Here are some things that worked for me, and who knows, they might work for you as well:

1. Time. You are not going to get there quickly. I joined my first Toastmaster (TM) group in 2012 deciding to conquer my fears, and you know what happened? My first speech was supposed to be 4 to 6 minutes, and even though I read most of it, it took me 13 minutes to finish. Thirteen, long, agonizing minutes... but you know what? At the end my face was red and sweaty, but inside I was glowing. I had done it! I said every single word I intended to say and nobody booed me. It was terrifying but I couldn't wait to do it again. If you want to get really good at ANYTHING you need time, a really long time, so you better start now.

2. Patience/Resilience. It's not going to go well right away so get yourself ready for some failures. I joined TM in 2012 but I quickly realized it was just not going to be a smooth road. Even though I loved it and my speeches were good when it came to content, my actual speech sucked. Deep down I knew I jumped into the deep end too quickly, so after less than a year I quit... AND THAT WAS A GOOD THING. I didn't quit on my dream; I just knew I wasn't ready. I needed some time to work on it but I was going to be back. Know that a failure is only a failure if you don't use it to move forward, be patient.

3. Friends. Surround yourself with people that care for you. I would not be trying so many crazy things if I didn't have so many friends that push me to go out of my comfort zone every single day. Friends that make fun of you, friends that hug you when you fail, friends that cheer you when you win. Surround yourself with love and you can do anything.

4. Find support. Similar to friends, but a little more specific. GET HELP. Find a local support group for people that stutter. The **NATIONAL STUTTERING ASSOCIATION** is there for you and they have chapters all over the country, I can't stress how important this is. My life changed the moment I stopped feeling alone and I realized I WAS NEVER ALONE, I JUST DIDN'T KNOW WHERE MY TRIBE WAS. If there is not a chapter close to you, you are still not alone, Stuttering Arena, Stuttering Community and Stuttering Hangout are just some of the groups on Facebook where you can find that support. Do it.

5. Find your inspiration. I went to my first stuttering conference in 2011 and I can't express how life changing that was. The very first person I met was this guy from Alabama named **Jody Fuller** and when I asked him what his profession was and he said comedian. PAUSE. Did he just say comedian? This guy was, to me, a walking epiphany. I had never met anybody like him and my life just couldn't be the same after that. He showed me that there truly was no limit, and that same message was repeated over and over at that conference. Doctor, architect, lawyer, pilot, comedian, CEO, vice president of the USA, actor... whatever you feel you can't be because of your stutter, YOU ARE WRONG, chances are somebody already did it before you... and if not, you are going to be the first, which is even better! Set your sight on that something you really want to be and start walking!

6. Challenge yourself. In the time between my first TM group in 2012 and the current one I joined in 2015 I worked as a host and later a server and manager at a restaurant, literally making a living by talking to strangers. I did karaoke for the first time. I told jokes on stage. I gave a one hour talk at a conference. I conducted meetings. I got involved with my stuttering group until I became the leader. I learned how to rap. I lost my fear of ordering at drive-thrus. At 32 years old I called my friends on the phone for the first time. I gave talks about stuttering at 3 universities. I started a business.... The more scared you are of doing something, the more you have to do it, and every challenge, no matter how small, adds to your confidence and builds momentum. Getting good at one thing is pretty much the same as getting good at anything... it's just practice and repetition, so be fearless and never stop looking for challenges.

And finally,

7. Set an insane goal and go for it. When I joined TM again in 2015 I looked for the biggest group I could find in the city and I set the bar at "become a world-class speaker". I told myself I was going to become the best, not in spite of my stuttering, but BECAUSE OF IT, I was going to embrace it... and guess what? I did it. Last Thursday I won my first speech contest with a 7-minute speech about stuttering.

So... what is that thing you have been running from? I say it's time to go for it. Let me know if I can help you, you are never alone.

www.ingramcontent.com/pod-product-compliance
Lightning Source LLC
Chambersburg PA
CBHW032123090426
42743CB00007B/446